OVER MY SHOULDER

OVER MY SHOULDER

A COLUMBINE SURVIVOR'S
STORY OF RESILIENCE, HOPE, AND A LIFE RECLAIMED

KACEY RUEGSEGGER JOHNSON

WITH KAREN BOOKER SCHELHAAS

Dedicated with all my love to Mallory Lynne,
Logan Jo, Bentley Mae, and Corban Patrick

CONTENTS

Foreword ix

CHAPTER 1
From The Floor 1

CHAPTER 2
Lacey Kacey 13

CHAPTER 3
The Dark Descent 22

CHAPTER 4
April 20, 1999 37

CHAPTER 5

Heroes 63

CHAPTER 6

My "New Normal" 88

CHAPTER 7

Tattoos Of Survival 127

CHAPTER 8

Just One More 162

CHAPTER 9

Letting Go 185

CHAPTER 10

Beauty From Ashes 196

CHAPTER 11

Over My Shoulder 214

Afterword 229

About AlloSource® 241

Acknowledgments 245

About the Authors 251

FOREWORD

I t is an honor and a privilege for me to introduce Kacey Ruegsegger Johnson. I have known Kacey for fourteen years, and I have heard her speak many times at events sponsored by AlloSource, a nonprofit tissue donation bank I have led for eighteen years. Each time Kacey shares her story, it evokes a variety of emotions in me. Her experiences bring me to tears, sometimes of sorrow and sometimes of joy, but she also makes me smile and laugh. More importantly, Kacey's story of triumph over great adversity brings me hope and encouragement.

I first met Kacey in Pasadena, California, on New Year's Eve in 2004. She was there with her parents and siblings; Kacey and her sister Britney were scheduled to ride on the Donate Life Float in the Rose Parade on New Year's Day. Severely injured in the 1999 Columbine High School shooting, Kacey was a recipient of donated bone and tissue used to reconstruct her right hand, arm, and shoulder. The Donate Life Float was part of a multiday celebration of both donor families and recipients. I must admit that I was nervous to meet and talk with her. I was simply unsure of what to say and how to carry on a conversation with someone who had been seriously injured in that horrific event.

Nevertheless, I met Kacey the day before the parade, and my nervousness quickly dissipated. Conversation with her was easy, although she seemed shy and somewhat scared to be in the spotlight. The surprising strength she possessed would not be obvious to me until that evening. Shortly after talking with her, I met the rest of her immediate family. I could not escape thoughts of my own sons as I spoke with them; I could only imagine the deep well of strength the Ruegseggers must have needed under such difficult circumstances. Greg and Darcey, Kacey's parents, were clearly her strong, protective shield, and her siblings, Brian, Britney, and Brett provided the kind of comic relief only brothers and sisters can. The whole family impressed me.

That evening, I saw Kacey's strength on full display. Five years after the shocking events at Columbine High School, speaking for the first time as a tissue recipient, Kacey stepped into the public eye at the Donate Life dinner reception. She did so reluctantly, not because she wanted attention (she clearly did not), but because she wanted to help others. Kacey stood in front of the large audience, a small figure behind the podium, and spoke alongside her sister with a quiet strength and poise that captivated the room. She talked beautifully about an experience most people cannot fathom, explaining the importance of the gift of donated tissue she had received. There was not a dry eye in the room. The "Donate Life" celebration became the foundation of our friendship; it was the first of many opportunities over the years for me to see Kacey openly sharing her life with others, creating hope and healing in the process.

During the years I have known her, I have learned of other equally difficult events in her life, both before and after the Columbine shooting. She is a survivor, but she is so much more than that. Kacey's story is complex in many ways, but for me it is simple in this sense—I have seen her blossom into a person of humility, grace, courage, and perseverance who is determined to use her life experiences to help other people.

I am confident that the hope and encouragement I feel every time I hear Kacey communicate her powerful message will be shared by each person who turns these pages.

—Thomas A. Cycyota,
   President and CEO,
   AlloSource
   Centennial, Colorado

CHAPTER 1

FROM THE FLOOR

*O*n *a sunny April day in Littleton, Colorado, I find myself sitting in the library at Columbine High School. New to the school as a seventeen-year-old junior, this is my first visit to the library. It is also the first time all year I have decided to stay at the school for lunch. Typically, I am in my car at this time driving home for the break, but instead I am reading a magazine: a stupid gossip magazine, no less. I notice that the large bright room is nicer than the library at my previous school; large double doors, long shelves lined with books, plenty of table space for studying and long rows of cubicles topped with big computers. A wall of windows frames the school's view of the Rocky Mountains. On my walk to the back of the room, I choose a cushioned chair near the windows and watch students in the parking lot leaving* *for off-campus lunch. Only minutes after making myself comfortable, I hear a popping noise outside the window. I turn my head to look, but I see nothing. I relax and focus on my magazine.*

A boy approaches the area where I am reading. He looks lost. I notice a lot because I rarely say anything. But I decide to talk on this day. I look up and feel prompted to say, "Hey, you can sit here." Five simple words destined to be forgotten, surely. A small gesture of kindness in an otherwise normal day. The boy sits down, clearly thankful for a spot to sit. For the rest of my life, I will remember us reading together quietly for those few minutes, two strangers inextricably linked by five words of invitation.

Then: "Get down, everybody down, get on the floor, and get DOWN!!" She is yelling, the teacher with a phone in her hand. "Get down, get your heads under the tables, and hide!!!!! There's a boy outside with a gun!"

When I hear a pop inside of the building, near the entrance to the library, I know. I recognize the sound from minutes earlier.

The speed of the blood pumping through my veins accelerates, coursing with fear and panic. I run, weightless, to hide in a cubicle under a computer table ten feet away, pulling a chair up to protect my exposed right side. There is nothing but flimsy particleboard on three sides of me, the lone chair acting as my defense against the unknown.

The boy reading next to me stands up more slowly, not knowing what to do. I tell him to get under a table, which he does, but he does not have a chair to protect him. In my mind, chairs seem to be important.

There is no time to think. I just act. The only prayer I utter: "God, HELP us. God, HELP."

My heart pounds loudly in my chest in these minutes; I shake uncontrollably. My ears become acutely attuned to sounds that might give me an idea of what's happening.

The teacher breathlessly yells again, "Get down, get under the tables, and get your heads DOWN!" She is also giving details to a 911 operator while her own shoulder drips blood onto the carpet.

The first shot enters the library. In what was a flurry of untrained teenagers finding refuge in an impending war zone, there is now a weird silence, lasting only seconds. I don't know for sure if the shot found its target.

I sense the shooters' presence before I can even see or hear them. Ahead of them, a darkness creeps in across the floor; a rushing sea of heaviness that feels like a physical punch to my gut, an evil compression.

"Everybody get UP! This is your day to die! We're going to blow this whole library up. Everybody with a white hat, get UP!" The jocks wear white hats. The shooters' voices are loud and calm. They are laughing, enjoying their command of the room. This has been carefully planned.

Nobody moves. Nobody is obedient. Pipe bombs are exploding and guns are firing. A computer is shot five feet from me. The explosion is incredibly loud and makes me cower lower to the floor.

I can't see anything, but my ears are trading places with my eyes and drawing me a map of the shooters' locations. Another prayer forms in my mind: "Please God, don't let them force me to stand up."

And then I experience what I have only heard about. My short life actually passes before my eyes. I see scrolling images of vacations with my siblings, of me and my younger sister, pictures of me and my two brothers, a snapshot of my parents, and of my horse, Moxie. They look like a photo album in my head, a slow-moving slideshow that my most deeply lodged memories have chosen for me to view.

I realize the shooters, who seem to be more agitated and focused now, are approaching me from the left side, moving stealthily around the library from left to right. I'm ten feet or so from the wall of windows, one of which is now shot out completely.

There's a sudden clamp on my back, a strong and steady hand. My first hurried thought is "Who on earth could possibly fit in this tiny cubicle with me?" It is the one moment of stillness in the dark symphony of gunshots. A hand is placed upon me moments before my body is forever altered. Its strong presence is so undeniably real, its grip so strong, that I glance over my left shoulder fully expecting to see someone. There is no one, of course. But then there is the whispered telling that I will be shot, the knowing for sure, the hand clearly attached to a messenger. I'm stilled by this intimate visit. I am alone, but I'm not. I've been forewarned of my impending injury or death. It is unmistakable in my head, not through a clear voice, but in a deep knowing that joins the blood in my throbbing veins. I am not told if I will live or die.

At this exact moment, I feel a spiritual shift in the general area of my stomach, and a peace descends. Its calming static in my ears will act as an aid to help me with what I'm hearing, sounds no young girl should ever hear. Terror continues to race through my veins, as though my blood has a fever. I'm hot. But my sense of panic is gone, replaced strangely with peace.

I hear continued gunfire. It's getting closer to me. One of the shooters walks past me and drops his trench coat on the floor, and I can tell by the clanking noise that he is laying a huge gun on the table next to me. The other shooter is now by the wall of windows where I had been sitting with the boy. My back is to him, my head facing the right wall of my cubicle.

I look over my right shoulder for the first time to get a visual of the shooters. One of them is crouching by the chair I was sitting in only minutes before.

He is hunching down, holding a large shotgun pointed at the boy behind me, the words he spoke to me moments ago destined to be his last. I immediately turn away and plug my ears because I know the blast will be deafening. And it is.

All I can think is that the boy doesn't have a chair. I do not know if he's dead or badly injured, but I know I will never forget this particular blast. I will never forget him.

I'm next.

The shooter doesn't move from his position and turns the shotgun on me. I hear the blast and feel myself being thrown forward, watching my right arm fly in slow motion out in front of me.

I feel nothing.

My head hits the wall of the cubicle and the blast shoves all the air out of my lungs. I make a guttural sound in the exhale that prompts the shooter to sneer, "Quit your bitching."

I go completely limp and close my eyes. The clarity in my mind is razor-sharp, maybe sharper than it's ever been. I need him to believe his work with me is finished. I know I've got to play dead in this sick game he is playing or he will win, and I will lose more than I have already lost.

Seconds later, I open my eyes and catch a glimpse of him turning the shotgun under another table to shoot a girl. I hear nothing, as I lay badly wounded under the cubicle desk. I shut my eyes when he turns the shotgun. I don't want to watch what is going to happen, and I do not want him to see that I am alive. I will not give him that pleasure.

While playing dead, I hear them taunt again, "If you're not going to get up, we are just going to come to you!" They are now targeting others with demeaning words and racial slurs.

The blasts ring out, one after the other. The floor beneath me is a glimmering crimson pool, all of us united in this red.

The room has gone quiet. The girl hiding in the cubicle next to me leans over the thin wall of particleboard and cautiously asks if I'm alive. "Yes," I say. She is not physically injured.

It is only now that the killers have moved past me that their rearrangement of my body becomes clearer. My throat begins to close and I feel like I cannot breathe. The slug from the shotgun shell has ripped through the back of my right shoulder, exiting near my collarbone and passing through my right thumb that is still instinctually plugging my right ear. It then burned a path across the front of my neck and hit my left hand which was still plugging my other ear. I am keenly aware that if the slug had traveled one more inch up, down, or sideways I would not be fighting to stay alive.

In this sudden battle to survive, it is not pain that I feel. Instead, it is a deep tightening in the muscles of my right arm and shoulder, an unbearable heaviness. I cannot move.

I glance over my right shoulder to see a gaping hole, only to then be distracted by the sight of my right thumb which seems to be pumping blood like a garden hose. With my bloodied left hand, I apply pressure to my right thumb. A pool of blood is collecting on the floor in front of me and I reach down, using my left index finger like a dipstick to try and measure it. The blood rises past my first knuckle. I measure it three times.

I'm immovable, but amazingly lucid. The tightening increases in my arm, and I sense that my body is contracting in an effort to close the hole surrounding my shattered bones and ruptured skin and shredded muscles. I feel like I'm suffocating.

The swelling in my throat from the lead slug's graze leads to an unquenchable thirst and very labored breathing. The shooters are gone now. It's eerily quiet and the air is heavy with echoes of the terror that has now passed us by.

A boy rises up out of a pool of blood from those shot dead next to him and yells, "Let's GO!" Survivors crawl out of their hiding places and start running to the exit-only door located on the west side of the library.

I know I cannot move on my own because I cannot push the chair out from underneath the cubicle. It is the first moment I cannot use my right arm, my first disabled moment. I'm keenly aware of it.

"Somebody help me get out!" I yell. I don't recognize my new, stronger voice.

The boy who has yelled at everyone to get out of the library hears my cry and moves the chair, somehow pulling me up to my feet. I cannot say how he does it. But he does.

I see the other boy then, the one who had been reading next to me and then hid in the cubicle behind me; I know that he is dead. I will be spared remembering the graphic imagery of the area around my hiding spot, but I have to step over his hand to exit the library.

The boy helping me is on my left side using his arm to hold my injured arm against my body. He does not know me; I do not know him. It strikes me that I am running, fleeing really, although I can't feel myself doing it. Everyone is stampeding. There are bodies left behind. This makes us run faster, the still living, hard-wired for freedom.

There are some rooms on the way to the exit-only door, and several kids are second-guessing their escape and instead staking out the first refuge they can find. The boy leading me out of the library yells at them to get out, and everyone follows his lead.

At the exit door, in the chaos, he loses his grip on me and I'm standing alone. I begin to run and use my bleeding left hand to hold my right arm tightly against my body, not knowing if it is going to fall off or not.

A group of about twenty students run with me out across the field and hide behind a police car. The policeman is pointing his gun at the school. The boys begin taking off their shirts and use them in an effort to stop the bleeding of their injured classmates. A girl I know from my church youth group is holding a boy's shirt to my shoulder to soak up the blood. She asks my name; I am surprised that she cannot recognize me.

Another police car rolls across the field to transfer injured students to the medical staff that is waiting on

9

residential streets. I am the first student along with another girl from this group of escapees to be taken for care. I ask my friend holding the shirt if she can join us. "No, the injured only," the policeman grunts.

I still don't feel safe.

The policeman drives me and the other girl a short distance to a shed where he stops and makes us get out again. We are sitting in the grass behind the shed, and my blood continues to track my movements on the ground, life leaking out. It is getting harder and harder to breathe. My arm is heavy and I feel like I cannot take one more step.

Five more minutes pass until the policeman comes back and tells us to get back into his car. I can't do it. I ask for his help. He doesn't help me. He seems frantic.

I somehow manage to stumble into the car and am halfway inside when, in his haste, he slams the door into my left shoulder, pushing me over on to my severely injured right shoulder. For a moment, I think to myself that he could have been a little more helpful. I'm trying to sit back up as he starts driving across the field. The ride feels bumpy and wild. I'm still clearheaded and pain free, unusually heavy feeling and every muscle is stretched tight, but not in pain. Not yet.

We arrive at a cul-de-sac in a nearby neighborhood that has been set up as a triage area. Again, no one helps me out of the car. I crawl out of the car and lay down in the grass a final time, utterly spent. Someone takes my picture. There are other injured classmates and a *flurry of strangers wanting to help us. Helicopters are flying overhead.*

A man comes up to me with a bulky cell phone and asks me whom he might call. I haven't received any medical attention yet, and a phone call feels insufficient, ridiculous. I give him my mom's number, though, and ask him for water. He brings me a garden hose.

A nurse races over and stops me from taking a drink, telling me I will be going straight into surgery. "Am I going to lose my arm?" I ask her.

I can tell by the hesitation in her voice that she can't speak with authority about it. She quietly repeats, "You will be going straight into surgery."

The man with the cell phone calls my mother and asks me if I can speak to her. "No," I say, because I know it will make me lose my resolve and I will fall apart. I'm a seventeen-year-old who's been in a war I wasn't equipped to fight, my only weapons a magazine, a chair, some flimsy particleboard, and a strong hand on my back. I cannot explain all this to my mother in this moment.

The paramedics arrive at my side and all I can think is how good looking they are. I am a teenage girl, after all. As they load me into the ambulance, I begin to feel pain. At this moment, the fight-or-flight instinct is quieted and I am able to feel the first visceral responses to my injuries. I have also lost a shoe, and I am a bit upset that it might be left behind. I'm bleeding to death, with an arm precariously anchored to a shoulder made cloud-like by the dust of my bones, and it is a shoe I think about.

This is all in real-time for me; never once have I left my body or my head to watch it happen to me from another place. The clarity is a refining fire, similar to the searing pain building a new heat in my body.

"When can I have pain medicine?" I ask the very calm men keeping watch over me.

"We're getting you there as fast as we can," one of them tells me. "You will get medicine in the ER. But first, we need to cut your clothes off to search for further injuries." Two good-looking men are going to cut my clothes off. My face is crimson, feeling their scissors slice through what is left of my dignity.

"Please, don't cut off my jeans. They're my favorite." This is all I say before I shrink back into my usual shyness. I am a timid girl, although no one would guess that about me if they had watched these last few minutes very carefully. But there are lots of minutes before where they would have known. Seventeen years of them, to be exact.

CHAPTER 2

LACEY KACEY

I see it now, as I look back to a precious time in my life. It is such a beautiful gift, a good and decent childhood: one filled with cookies on the counter, clean laundry and homemade dinners, school pick-ups, parents who waited up for midnight chats, and ever-present siblings. My home was a warm refuge of comfort and security, and that built great resolve in my bones. It was no small thing, those seventeen years I spent in purposeful preparation.

I'm not a firstborn, but I act like one at times. I'm the second of four children, arriving on March 29, 1982, all green-eyed, blonde, and freckled at the dawn of big hair, leg warmers, and heavy-metal bands. My brother Brian is four years older than I am; he can command a room with his high energy, handsome looks, and gregarious personality (traits that will benefit him in his future career as an attorney). My sister Britney is two years younger, bubbly and social to my stoic and shy. Brett, born two years after Britney on the same day, is four years younger than me and forever the baby of the family, fiercely wielding his hockey stick and keeping us laughing. I am the lone introvert sailing through a sea of extroverted siblings.

My mom and dad, Greg and Darcey Ruegsegger, met in high school and married years later in Colorado, a marriage that has withstood the tests of time and has brought both of them great joy. They defer to each other's strengths, and give each other plenty of space to be who they are without judgment. It's an excellent relationship model, and I've been privy to a front-row seat.

My mother, the youngest of three children, fearlessly roamed the heavily wooded outdoors, hunting and fishing during her childhood in Flushing, Michigan. She loved horses, referring to them as her best friends, but had a special connection with Champ, a quarter horse she used to ride bareback for hours. I'm genetically hard-wired to love horses because of her. Mom's independent spirit was established early, her soul anchored in a deep reservoir of strength and faith that has served her well.

Dad had humble beginnings in Canada, one of ten children born to a pastor and his wife in Three Hills, Alberta, nearly eighty miles north of Calgary. He's a natural leader and a competitive athlete who plays hockey to this day. His family moved south to Flushing, Michigan, in his sophomore year of high school. Dad later attended and played football and baseball at Taylor University in Indiana and went to the University of Colorado for law school.

In light of future events, my childhood can only now be appreciated as idyllic and carefree. I was given very sure footing in the world, despite my often-hesitant steps toward maturity.

Most of my early days were spent in Lakewood, Colorado. "Lacey Kacey" made her debut in those days, a very tiny girl riding the rocking horse at church with wild abandon, dressed in an all-white lace dress that my dad's Canadian friend had sent as a gift. I spent hours playing dress-up with my sister, but we had equal measures of roughhousing with our brothers in the beautiful Colorado outdoors. In the few instances I needed discipline, my parents just had to look at me sideways to change my behavior. I was not a difficult child.

With daily devotion, Mom drove us around town to school and various activities. Dad worked long hours as a litigation attorney, arriving home most nights for tickle fights on the floor with me and my sister, her jumping into the chaos while I usually retreated, ever thoughtful and shy.

My dad has always been my hero. We once spent a week exploring New York City when I was in the sixth grade. We saw *Cats* on Broadway while we were there, quite an experience for a quiet girl who certainly did not enjoy crowds. There was so much snow piled up. Even though I was timid, my dad gave me the strength I needed to stand on top of a huge snowdrift, the skyline of the city twinkling in the distance. There I was, beaming for a picture that depicted a girl defiantly standing tall with the world at her back.

I was raised in a Christian home, but my parents taught us that our relationship with God is a deeply personal one. We were on one of many family road trips when I decided to accept Jesus as my Savior at the age of eight. My dad was driving that night and the rest of the family was asleep behind us. My conversion was a sacred moment I treasure, a quiet prayer exchanged with God as my dad listened. A few weeks later, Dad had the privilege of baptizing Britney and me, formally proclaiming our intimate internal decisions to the outside world. It was a life-changing moment for me, this choice to welcome salvation from God, and one I've never regretted. My relationship with Him has always brought great life to my soul; I know I'm never alone.

I was never suffocated by long theological debates at the dinner table or forced to attend church three times a week. I caught far more than I was ever taught through the attitudes and actions of my parents. We were immersed in faith without drowning in it. Our community at Cornerstone Church, and later at Southern Gables Church, just up the street from Columbine High School, were churches that taught us the Bible and modeled the importance of serving others.

Even though I was given every advantage as a child, I was often unsure of myself in public. My parents had some concerns. When my sister and I sold Girl Scout cookies, I'd send Britney to the door and wait near the street while she did the cold calling, knocking on doors with the social confidence I couldn't quite muster. On Halloween, I'd send her up the sidewalk while I kept to the shadows, hoping she could get our orange buckets filled with candy I would rather live without than ask for.

My parents worried the world might be cruel to such a shy young girl. I used to hide behind their legs, eyes averted to the ground, and I was virtually mute in social settings. So, at the age of seven, after it became clear that I did not love team sports, my parents bought my first horse, an Arabian named Shazeer. We boarded him at a stable near our home. My mom wanted to expose me to a sport where I might inch my way toward a self-assurance that would resonate in the world outside the sanctuary of my home and family.

My sister and I started spending extended time at the barn. We began riding lessons and taking care of the horses by cleaning the straw-filled stalls, feeding them, and brushing their silky coats. I had an immediate bond with the animals, much like my mother did at that age. I knew it was what I wanted to do, and where I wanted to be. There was a heart connection I couldn't quite explain. At the same time, I was enrolled in competitive gymnastics, excelling in floor, tumbling, and uneven bars; I was fully devoted to both disciplines.

Shazeer was sold rather quickly when we realized that Arabian horses weren't the standard for horse shows in which I found myself wanting to compete, and so we made the move to quarter horses. We were incredibly busy, every night of the week. At the ages of eight and ten, my sister and I took our new horses to 4-H at the Jefferson County Fairgrounds and learned about their care and the vocabulary of the equestrian world. My parents hired riding instructors at the barn that helped us gain the skills we needed to ride properly. Despite some hard falls at the beginning of my equestrian career, I kept getting back up. I began to have a lot of success, and I loved it. I discovered my inherited competitive streak riding those horses, my will to win propelling me forward. My mom's plan was working.

My multiple 4-H victories led to my entrance into serious competition, transitioning into American Quarter Horse Association (AQHA) events at the age of twelve. With that jump came the need to upgrade my horse again and an investment in a higher-level trainer. I cherished my time with each of my horses but recognized that equestrian competition was also a business. Saying goodbye was hard, but each horse I sold went to a good home; my family made sure of that. We began competing all over the state of Colorado. I won more events than I lost. A newly-minted teenager with increasing confidence, I spent all my time at the barn.

Weekend horse events involve showing seven disciplines, some of which focus on the horse's movement and others that concentrate on the rider's precise position through a predetermined pattern. Whether under an English or Western saddle, the connection between horse and rider is essential for success. Equestrians can choose to be an expert at one discipline, or they can decide to be an All-Around athlete who shows all seven disciplines. I chose the All-Around and even though it was my goal to win that award, I still wanted to win "high point" for each discipline. While my sister often socialized at weekend events, I was most often found in the barn, fiercely training for competition. My trophy case was filling up.

By my freshman year of high school, I had to choose between gymnastics and horses. With great ease, I chose horses and never looked back. I had such a deeply rooted relationship with the powerful animals, my heart inextricably intertwined with life at the barn. My social confidence, as my mother predicted, was steadily growing in tandem with my success at equestrian events. I competed at the state level for a year, and my trainer was a joyful, kind, and gentle woman named Julie. Most of my trainers were like family to me.

My parents and I made the decision to move to national competition during my freshman year of high school. My horse at the time was a male named Moxie, a buckskin-colored quarter horse with a yellow body and black points. Instead of vacations spent visiting relatives, as we used to do, now all our family time away from home was spent at equestrian events as well as my brother Brett's hockey games all over the country. It was a remarkable time in the life of our family.

As a family, we decided to engage Chad and Barbie Evans, professional trainers at a new barn in Parker, Colorado. It was a decision I led, but my parents supported. These trainers had excellent results and trustworthy relationships with equestrians my age. My sister and I practiced every night after school for three hours, and nearly every weekend in the summer was spent at competitions. Winter was a season of more intense training, but also included weekend sleepovers and dance parties at the trainers' house. Everyone training at the same barn competed against each other, so these laughter-infused gatherings helped to maintain fun and camaraderie. One training event involved ten one-dollar bills. Chad and Barbie would line us up on our horses without saddles to perfect our riding seat position. If the dollar fell out from underneath our pinned knees, the trainers kept the money. We got to keep the money if we had great position and didn't drop it; I was a rich girl!

Right before we joined Chad and Barbie's team, my parents bought a new house in Littleton, Colorado, with five acres of land, and built a brand-new 2,500 square-foot horse barn on the property. The barn was already constructed before we realized that the level at which my sister and I were going to compete required us to keep our horses at the trainers' barn. Our family barn became a boardinghouse for other people's horses and also was home to our noncompetitive family horse. Our family still giggles over the bad timing.

All of those years of childhood were stairs headed up to the new heights I would climb, my shyness only faintly recognizable when looking back over my shoulder. But there was a low to which I would plummet first, a low no one saw coming. It swallowed me up as quickly as it would later spit me out.

CHAPTER 3

THE DARK DESCENT

When I graduated from Bear Creek Middle School in 1996, my mom had strong reservations about enrolling me at Bear Creek High School. Even though my older brother, Brian, attended the same school, she worried that I might get lost in the large crowd of two thousand students. She nevertheless let me register, and my freshman year was mostly uneventful which calmed my mother's fears. It was also the year when I made the move to national equestrian competition, and our family was out of town most weekends enjoying the sport we loved.

I loved my weekly youth group at Southern Gables Church and looked forward to my interactions with my youth pastor. All of my social activities up to that point revolved around the innocence my childhood had afforded me. My faith was secure, my family a great comfort, and

I had a place to belong at the barn and at church. I lacked very little, if anything at all.

At the beginning of my sophomore year, a shift occurred in me, quite subtly at first. Intrigued by a good-looking group of athletes, mostly boys, I began hanging out on the fringes of their crowd at school. It wasn't calculated but born of a natural curiosity and a desire to fit in at school. This new affiliation with the popular crowd now held my attention.

One guy stood out from the rest. His name was Mark. He had stunning looks, a bright mind, and was well-liked by most of the students at our school. His older brother was a star athlete, and Mark was always striving to reach his brother's potential. We spent countless hours together, building a close friendship sprinkled with a healthy dose of attraction. However, there was some tension between us that often gave me pause, and I knew it would ultimately cause problems in our relationship.

My parents began wondering who exactly was influencing whom in this new group of friends. My mom remembers the little things that changed in me at first, like the tone in my voice and my lack of respect. She sensed what felt like the deep pleasure of God disappearing in my life. I started withdrawing from my family, clamming up, cooling the familial warmth. That led to typical teenage secretive behavior, wounding my parents and siblings in the process. I unintentionally built a wall between my family and me, one brick of discontent at a time. Without much thought, I turned almost all my attention to my new group of friends.

On March 8, 1998, our family arrived home from one of my brother Brett's hockey games in Vail, Colorado. I marched into the kitchen to our answering machine to retrieve what I hoped would be several messages about my presence being missed at social events that weekend. There was a lone message from a friend, saying something was wrong with Mark. I ran up to my bedroom and swiftly dialed his home number. His brother answered the phone.

"Is Mark there?"

"No. You haven't heard?"

"No. What?"

"Mark's dead. He hung himself last night."

Hung himself last night. Dead. Mark. I went into shock. Piercing, wailing screams formed in my throat, fueled by emotions I didn't know I had. My parents bolted upstairs to find me writhing inconsolably on the floor. After spending a couple of hours trying to get me to calm down, they eventually called my best friend from the barn, Lindsay ("Spike"), and asked her to spend the night with me at our house. She was like a sister to me and a third daughter to my parents. Her presence was definitely helpful in the midst of my grief.

Mark and I had been in literature class together in the fall, reading *The Scarlet Letter*. I remembered him saying in front of the whole class, "I'm going to hang myself someday!"

I quickly replied, "No, Mark. No, you won't!" And I giggled. We all giggled. That response would haunt me for years.

Mark had often mentioned that I wouldn't be seeing him much after basketball season. I didn't understand what he was saying, of course, and brushed off his strange comments. But I knew a lot was weighing heavily on him. So heavily, it turned out, that he drove home from the end-of-season basketball party and hanged himself.

He died on a Sunday, and I went to school on Monday, finding great solace in my new group of friends. We understood each other, or at least we thought we did, whispering words of comfort punctuated with growing discontent. At first, my grief seemed appropriate to my parents, but I quickly slid into a deep depression. My limbs, my eyelids, they all felt so heavy. I had visions of Mark hovering over my bed, dark images racing through my mind. I threw myself into the chaotic sea of teen angst, waves of emotion gaining momentum. There was a lot of talk with my friends about death, and finding comfort in destructive things. My friends and I left our parents out of the grief equation entirely despite their desperate attempts to reach us. I opted to go to parties with my friends instead of going to my youth group, and that decision shut the light out of my life completely.

My sixteenth birthday fell at the end of March, and after getting my license, I sold my parents a story about driving my new friends to youth group, which I had no intention of doing. We landed on Lookout Mountain instead, in the beautiful foothills of Denver, eager to find comfort in each other's misery.

I wrote a note to my friends at school about our activities that night, and shoved it in my jeans pocket without much thought. Later that week, taking a big risk, I invited the group to my house to hang out in the basement. My parents kept their reservations to themselves, thankful that I'd invited the kids into our home. As I was entertaining them, my mom was simultaneously doing laundry in the laundry room and discovered the incriminating note. My parents' fears were realized. References to the use of drugs and alcohol left no doubt. I never participated in any of it, but I had willingly let my friends' activities begin to feel like normal behavior; it began to inch me toward a new identity my family didn't recognize.

My mother hurried to show my dad the note. After reading it, he called me out of the basement into their bedroom. Believe it or not, this was the first time I ever really got in trouble, and the confrontation was devastating to me. They instructed me to read the letter aloud to them. I couldn't lie; I felt such shame. This was an added grief for my parents.

My dad took some time to gather his thoughts, then went down to the basement and confronted my group of friends, stating in very clear but loving language that lying, drugs, and alcohol were never going to be tolerated in his house. Everyone left eventually except for one girl who stayed to listen to my dad's heartfelt views about honesty. (As an attorney, he is very persuasive.)

Late that night, one of the boys came back to the house, and apologized to my dad, promising him he wanted to be a truthful person. In a goodwill gesture, he handed my dad a plastic baggie full of marijuana that he had been concealing in his jeans. My dad thanked him and put the bag in his own jacket pocket.

It wouldn't be until the next morning when my dad and mom were at my younger brother's school conference that he recalled placing it there. Sitting in the school office, he reached into his jacket, and suddenly remembered the pot he had been given the night before. He immediately fled the school with my mom at his heels, my straight-laced father, face burning red with embarrassment. My mother dissolved in fits of laughter in the parking lot. My parents rolled their eyes and laughed as they flushed it down the toilet later that day. It was a short and welcome break from the heaviness that now permeated our home.

I had been raised in a pretty sheltered environment and was very naive about worldly things going into high school. The challenging part for my parents was that they never saw this rebellion coming because I had been so "easy" to raise. The change in me was profound and quick, and they were ill-prepared to react to any of it. Their compliant, tender child became an angry, withdrawn teenager seemingly overnight. They never thought I was a "bad" kid, but just viewed me as a teenager struggling to find myself. They were not happy about a lot of my choices, but thought I would sort things out in the end.

Mere weeks after Mark's funeral, his best friend Luke, who was also a part of my group of friends, was on the phone with his girlfriend and suddenly told her "good-bye." We soon learned that he had walked to the garage of his home and hanged himself. His mother found him hanging there, a shattering external picture of the dark struggle in his soul. Luke was buried right next to Mark in the Golden Cemetery. As teenagers, those of us left behind to grieve were in a trance from all-too-familiar emotions that we were certainly not equipped to handle. Luke's funeral was on Friday; by Saturday, my parents knew I was in deep trouble.

Celine Dion's song *My Heart Will Go On* played incessantly through my speakers as I sat silently in my room journaling and drawing pictures of my two dead friends. A new plan was hatching to remove myself entirely from the frightening pain that had a chokehold on my life. I think my parents sensed the shift in me. On Monday morning they dragged me to a suicide counselor.

I refused to speak. The man, though I'm sure highly qualified, infuriated me and made me want to escape. Confused and overwhelmed, I said nothing, increasing my parents' anxiety. On Tuesday, I ran. A friend and I skipped school; he helped me put an impulsive plan together. I'd hang myself in our barn at 3:00 p.m. the following Sunday.

Thank God for my dearest friend, Spike. As soon as she got wind of my plan from our mutual friend, she called my parents and told them I was talking about suicide. Her wisdom probably saved my life, as I had laid down whatever sense of rationality I had at my friends' gravesites. My parents called the suicide counselor, and he sternly told them to "act like parents." It was confirmation of what my parents already knew. By Tuesday night, my life was no longer my own.

My parents' faces were as solemn as I had ever seen them. My dad looked right at me and said, "Kacey, listen clearly. We're pulling you out of school and you're not going to go anywhere alone. You'll sleep on a mattress in our room. You may not shut the bathroom door. The phone is off limits. And we don't care if you don't like it." All my freedom, snuffed out in six sentences. Even though I fought their rescue, I was aware I needed it.

On Wednesday morning, my folks drove me to the family doctor, another professional to whom I refused to speak. In an effort to shake my silent resolve, he asserted his authority. "Kacey, I can place you in a three-day psych hold at the hospital if you'd like, or you can cooperate with your parents." As angry as I was at the world, and all the while using my parents as a punching bag, I strangely did not want to be removed from their safety net. Their security was familiar, unlike anything a hospital would offer me, and I nodded to the doctor that I would cooperate.

We ended up at breakfast, my parents and me, and despite my lack of words, I ate more at that meal than I'd eaten in weeks. My dad took that as a sign that I was relinquishing control, my white flag waving with each forkful of food.

I avoided conversation with my parents for six weeks. For days, I laid in silence on a mattress in their room, fuming at the world. Finally, a few weeks into my silence, my parents let me return to youth group, driving me there and then home again. One night, my concerned youth pastor staged a meeting at one of my friend's homes, hoping to get a grasp on the pervasive darkness hovering over our troubled group. Devastated by the pain of our friends' deaths and deeply confused, we congregated in the basement continuing our talk about suicide while our parents sat upstairs despairing with the pastor. We were normal teenagers who wanted very little input from our parents, even in the midst of dealing with abnormal circumstances. We elected a spokesman from our group who trudged upstairs to let our parents know that we were handling our grief in our own way; he told them not to worry about us even though we all knew it was a lie.

When we returned home from the meeting, I received a call from one of the boys in the group. I knew he was in trouble. He was breathless. "Kacey, I'm up on Lookout Mountain and I'm going to kill myself." Since my parents were in the room listening to the conversation (I was not allowed to take phone calls alone), they immediately flew into crisis mode, calling every parent they knew. Our group of friends got in their cars and went to the mountains in search of him. I stayed on the phone with him for two hours, desperately trying to keep him calm. He eventually got help, thanks to another parent who was a police officer. That night was a marker, though. I would be blamed for this boy's downslide because he was interested in me romantically, and I did not return his advances. My group was desperate for someone to blame; I became the scapegoat for their anger. They eventually started to push me out of their circle, and I held my parents responsible for it and refused to speak to them.

My parents allowed me to return to school after three long weeks at home, but with strict instructions to avoid that group of friends entirely. They let me know in no uncertain terms they would be monitoring my activity at school. I went back and was shunned from the group, shattering what was left of my self-esteem, alienated by loneliness at school and at home. My mom described the final weeks of my silence. "I felt as if I was standing at the top of a big, black vortex and hanging on to Kacey with my fingertips. I felt a heavy blanket of darkness over our home, a massive departure from all that once was."

My siblings watched helplessly. Most of the burden fell on my thirteen-year-old sister, Britney. My refusal to eat had transformed my otherwise healthy body into a skeleton, my clothes now hanging off of my tiny frame. I was gaunt, pale, and detached; all of it scared her. Before my parents took control of my life, I would make Britney cover for me so I could spend time with my destructive friends. She was afraid of potential backlash from that group because of notes she had found while rummaging through my stuff. They were full of terribly wounding, angry words. She never told my mother about those notes or my true whereabouts, and she lived with a lot of fear as a result. Years later, she described it this way, "I remember our whole family shutting down, solely focused on keeping Kacey alive. The emptiness in her eyes, the lack of laughter or smiles, and all her anger were terrifying. I missed the old Kacey, my partner at the barn and at competitions all over the country. I craved normalcy."

My younger brother, Brett, watched my mother pre-emptively clean out our medicine cabinets one afternoon. On the way to hockey practice that night, he asked my dad, "Is someone in our family going to die?" Some of my dad's childhood friends from Canada visited during my enduring silence, and my mom fled to the basement in tears—there was no pretending. My parents felt that my descent threatened to change the beautiful landscape of our family once and for all.

But my dad; my wonderful dad. Every night, without fail, he dragged his heavy heart down the stairs to my bedroom where I was now allowed to sleep after spending three weeks in my parents' room. He would ask a million questions, all of which I refused to answer. Still, he kept trying to get through to me, spending hours just being in my presence. This constant pursuit of me during my months of misery led to an incredibly intimate relationship that would allow my dad to emotionally support me unlike anyone else after Columbine. He never once gave up on his little girl.

And my ever-faithful mom. She took the night watch and would check on me five to ten times in the middle of the night, going up and down the stairs, just to make sure I was safe and asleep. She made all my favorite foods in an effort to get me to eat, a silent offering. My parents spent countless hours on their knees begging God for healing for me, relentless in their quest to pull me back up onto my feet.

So, six long weeks later, I finally came back. I walked up the stairs, knocked on my parents' bedroom door, and quietly said, "I need to talk." And as swiftly as the ominous clouds had blown into my life, they blew out. My friends at youth group and my youth pastor had begun to pry open the door of my heart by listening and believing the best about me. That night, on the foot of my parents' bed, I shared all my emotions, heartaches, and sadness. They listened and cried in relief but asked nothing of me. I felt the shift in me physically, the heaviness being dragged away. Only God can do that. My mom says it was the year that God took me down to the studs and rebuilt me from the ground up. She was right.

I had a beautiful summer ahead of me, full of equestrian competitions. With my heavy sophomore year of high school finally behind me, I felt infused with new light and happiness. My parents breathed easier at night, and our family life returned to normal, albeit slowly.

But I had another friend from Bear Creek High School, Andy, who developed leukemia quite suddenly. We had crushes on each other in sixth grade; I was good friends with his sister at the barn. He even brought me a necklace once and left it in my tack box. He should have been fine with treatment, but the chemo gave him ulcerated sores in his throat. Those sores led to a terrible infection, and he died of sepsis. My parents went on hyper-alert, sure that his death would plunge me back into the dark abyss of grief, but I handled it very differently. I hurt, of course, and I mourned as they laid him near Luke and Mark in the same cemetery I had visited countless times. But I did not grieve as one with no hope. Andy had been attending youth group that summer and I was hopeful that he had started a relationship with Jesus. There was a marked difference in my response to yet another death, thanks to healthy supporting relationships and a faith that had really become my own.

I announced that I needed a fresh start. I asked to transfer to Columbine High School for my junior year. It was a comfortable and natural fit, with friends from church who attended there, as well as my best friend, Spike. We spent the majority of our junior year driving back to my house every day for lunch with my mom, chattering about boys and horses over sandwiches and cookies. I was a good student, but my real focus was on getting to the Quarter Horse World Show in Fort Worth, Texas, the following August. Leading several events in the state of Colorado at the time, I was at the height of my game.

I visited Mark's gravesite on the one-year anniversary of his death, and I know it worried my family. However, I didn't relapse into depression, as they feared I might. My faith was an anchor, and God was faithful to protect me from another downward spiral.

Julie had been my dearly loved horse trainer for part of my junior year. But after developing leukemia and going through rigorous treatments and a bone marrow transplant, it was necessary for her to step away from training. One day, she showed up at my parents' home rather unexpectedly for a friendly visit; my mom felt like Julie knew the end was near. She died suddenly on April 7, 1999, after her body rejected the bone marrow transplant. Her passing came exactly one year to the date of Luke's death. It was my fourth funeral in just over a year. As with Andy's death, I did not dip back into depression and a struggle with suicidal thoughts. Instead, I held onto the new beams of strength God had placed in my life. I wept over Julie's death, but once again handled my emotions in a way that did not worry my mom and dad. Still, my folks never rested from their watchful care over me.

On Sunday, April 18, I won my second All-Around Championship of the season. I was on my way to representing Colorado at the World Championships in Texas in August just as I had planned. I even opted out of going to the Columbine prom so I could compete that weekend. Monday was a rest day after such a strenuous weekend but I went to my job as a hostess at a local restaurant that night.

Tuesday was the twentieth. April 20, 1999. I got up and went to school.

CHAPTER 4

APRIL 20, 1999

*I*t's 6:15 a.m. I greet the early hour as I do every morning, fully awake and ready for another day. I spent last night at my hostess job at Lone Star Steakhouse. My parents and Spike came in to eat while I worked, and it helped the time to pass quickly. Walking to the bathroom, I realize I'm still a bit sore from last weekend's equestrian competition. I hop in the shower and then slip on my favorite jeans and a comfy white tank top. After a quick check in the mirror, I'm satisfied; I'm feeling cute and light. My moment on the medal stand from just forty-eight hours prior is replaying in my head, and I grin again, knowing that the All-Around Championship trophy I won is inching me closer to my goal of the World Championships in August. I will get there. I can feel it. Moxie and I are going to be ready.*

I select some fun, strappy sandals out of my closet for the day, noticing that Colorado's gorgeous sunshine is already trickling in through my basement windows and that it might be unseasonably warm for April, something to celebrate. I hate the cold and detest winter, and I'm thankful I get to wear my favorite things today—a tank top and sandals. Spring is ushering in a new landscape, and the earth just smells different this time of year. It's bursting with new growth, and my early morning mood matches the budding bushes and trees outside, full of new life. It's going to be a great day.

I bound upstairs and grab the cereal out of the pantry, snatch the milk out of the fridge and plop down at the breakfast table for my morning ritual of scouring the sports pages of the Denver Post *and the* Rocky Mountain News. *It's hard to find a bigger Avalanche hockey fan than me. I pride myself in knowing each player by name and all their stats. Plus, I have a crush on a couple of them, Peter Forsberg in particular. My sixth-grade brother, Brett, appears just then and says, "Hey Kacey. Hope you have a good day." I pat his blonde head and smile, wondering if this boy will change the game of hockey someday, his determination as strong and willful as mine.*

As I take my last bite of cereal, my dad appears and greets me as he sits down to eat his breakfast. The two of us like to eat and read our newspapers in companionable silence every morning. I throw my bowl and spoon in the sink, grab my backpack, and head out the door toward my Ford Explorer.

But wait.

Mom.

We aren't very touchy-feely, my mom and I, and we're not overly emotional with each other. But I feel an urge to go back inside the house as I stand on the doorstep of the garage. So, I do.

"Hey Mom! I love you!" I shout. "I love you, too, Kace!" she hollers back. And then I'm off to school, catching a glimpse of the early spring tulips beginning to blossom on our beautiful, five-acre horse property.

The drive to school is completely ordinary, traffic moving along as it usually does. I pass by Clement Park, noticing its new greenish hue as spring arrives, my favorite color on full display. Enough with winter and all the gray! I hope NSYNC's Bye Bye Bye *will play on the radio before I get to school, or maybe Faith Hill's* Breathe. *She's so lucky to be married to Tim McGraw! I turn right onto Pierce Street and approach Columbine High School.*

I pull into the southwest parking lot next to the cafeteria and park my Explorer. I walk up the west stairs, pass through the double doors, and arrive at the locker I share with Spike, which is just past the library. I drop my stuff off and head to math class.

The bell rings and I make my way to history class, wondering when I might see Spike to discuss our lunch plans. Every single day we find our way out to the parking lot and drive to my house to enjoy my mom's warm cookies and a light lunch, chattering about equestrian competitions, our life together at the barn, and darn cute hockey players. Maybe we will even get to sit outside and work on our tans today. With the sunshine beckoning me outside, it's hard to stay focused in class. Let's go already.

Spike and I ALWAYS meet at our locker at the start of the lunch hour, but today she does not show up. So, I walk to her math class to see if she is still in the classroom. She isn't. It's because of this unusual path, this searching for her that I don't normally have to do, that I end up walking by the library en route to my car. I suddenly realize I will not have time to get home and back again before my next class, so after I eat a granola bar, I decide to waste some time instead. It is my first time to enter the Columbine library all year.

The wall of windows on the west side of the library beckons me, and I quickly notice the clouds gathering over the foothills, knowing that a change in the weather, so typical for April, is headed our way. As they say, if someone doesn't like the weather in Colorado, just wait five minutes! My sandals will seem a silly choice when the snow flurries start, I think. I head to a cushioned chair near the windows to read a gossip magazine and wait for the lunch hour to pass.

I hear something. Pop. Pop. Pop. I look up, but I don't see anything.

I'm no longer alone in this reading area. There is a boy who has taken a seat next to me, at my invitation. He and I are quietly reading and waiting until we can head to our next class. I'm wondering where on earth Spike is today, and why she blew me off for lunch. I hope she's okay.

I hear the panicked teacher first. She's shouting actually, a phone stuck to her ear. Students begin to look worried, and people are starting to move around. What's happening? Is something wrong?

And then, those eight minutes. Those. Eight. Life. Altering. Minutes.

After my rescue from the library floor and subsequent exit from the war zone, I am soaked in my own blood, nearly naked, staring up into the faces of good-looking men helping me into the ambulance. Pieces of my shoulder and hand are left behind somewhere on the floor of the Columbine library.

The searing, hot pain is starting to radiate through my body as the ambulance rushes me toward the hospital. The sirens are screaming at confused drivers to get out of the way. I ask for pain medication, but I don't really ask with words as the minutes pass; it is more of a groaning than anything. I'm desperate to feel safe. I want my family.

There are phones ringing out across town now like an alarm, distress signals that something is terribly wrong at my high school. There is no protocol to follow in this chaos, no way to process it. The policeman who slammed the door into me, knocking me over onto my injured shoulder in the back seat of his squad car, made that glaringly obvious.

At home, my mom is spending her time doing chores and running errands, but she knows if she leaves she might miss Spike and me. Instead, she decides to bake us some oatmeal chocolate chip cookies, always excited about any moments she gets to have with her teenagers and their friends. She senses she really needs to be home.

My dad has spent the morning at the office before he heads to a quick business lunch around 11:00 a.m. He meets a colleague at a restaurant north of downtown Denver.

At 11:10 a.m., my mom notices that Spike and I are late for lunch but she puts the cookies in the oven anyway. When the timer goes off, she opens the oven door and grabs the tray while glancing at the clock. It's 11:30 a.m. She drops the cookies on the open oven door. Wait. Something's happening. She doesn't know if it has anything to do with me or not, but she knows something is wrong. Every cell in her body screams at her that something is not right. We're never late to lunch.

I am shot at 11:32 a.m.

On a hunch, my mom goes to the TV shortly thereafter, turns it on and immediately hears a voice say, "There are guns and bombs at Columbine High School." She knows in that moment that I'm involved. She drops to her knees in prayer. "God, be WITH her!"

My mom races to the phone and calls my dad's office. She can't reach anyone on the first try. She picks up the receiver and tries again despite her rising panic. Janet, my dad's receptionist, finally answers the phone.

"Janet, I REALLY need to find Greg."

"He's away at a meeting, Darcey."

"Okay," my mom says, and hangs up.

No, no. Wait. She calls back again.

"Janet, I have to find Greg. Find him, Janet. NOW!"

My mom runs outside to the driveway and everything within her wills my black Explorer to come zooming up the driveway. But she knows I'm not coming. She knows; her heart sinks inside her chest.

She goes back into the house to call my Aunt Catherine, my dad's sister-in-law, and tells her that she's terrified something has happened to me. Aunt Catherine says she will be right over to the house and that they will go to the school together. My mom says she can't leave the house. She knows the phone is going to ring. She's pleading with God, "Please be with her! PLEASE be with her. I can't be with her, so you have to be WITH her!!!"

Janet finally gets in touch with my dad. "Darcey called and said she needs to find you. You'd better call her immediately." Dad pays his bill and walks outside to his car. He calls my mom using his cell phone.

She's screaming and throwing out words like "bomb" and "guns" and he can't understand her completely.

"What are you talking about?!" he half-yells back.

43

"Greg, there are bombs and guns at Columbine and it's on TV and Kacey didn't come home for lunch and I know she's hurt!"

"No, Darcey. There are two-thousand kids at that school and after the year we have had with her, it CAN'T be her." It just can't, *he thinks.*

He gets in the car, speeding toward home. He considers not stopping at any stoplights. The voices on his car radio confirm my mom's words and his worst fears. There is something awful happening at Columbine. It's about 11:40 a.m.

My dad calls my mom again. Still, no news. They hang up the phone and Dad continues his long drive home, his knuckles turning white from his vice-grip on the steering wheel.

At 11:45 a.m., and just as my mother predicts, the phone rings in our kitchen. My mom is sure this is "the call." She picks up the receiver with trembling hands.

"Kacey?" a man's voice asks.

"No, I'm Darcey. Are you with Kacey?"

"Yes, I'm with Kacey. You need to get here fast."

"Is she okay?" my mom asks.

"She's hurt badly, and you have to get here." She can tell by the tone in his voice that he is very upset. He's talking way too fast.

My mom blurts, "Let me talk to her."

"You can't."

My mom immediately thinks I'm dead or unconscious. His words to my mom are "You can't" instead of "She won't" which is what I actually communicated to him; in the heat of the moment, he responds in error. There's a very wide gap of meaning between those words into which my mother is flung blindly.

He tries to explain our location, saying something about a cul-de-sac off Peakview. Out of the deep recesses of her memory, my mom remembers my brother Brett having a soccer game somewhere off Peakview years ago. She thinks she can get herself there. "I'm on my way," she says, and hangs up the phone just as Aunt Catherine walks in the door. My mom tells her they have to go immediately; Aunt Catherine says she will drive. My mom is wearing her dirty barn clothes as they speed out of the driveway. My dad is ten minutes away from home.

Mom and Aunt Catherine drive south on Kipling Parkway toward Peakview, and my mom calls my dad to tell him that she got a call from a man who says I'm hurt badly and that I can't talk to her.

My dad redirects his route and heads south on Wadsworth. They're both on a wild mission to get to me. But I'm already in an ambulance on Peakview; there are good-looking men watching over me, doing all they can to save my life in the midst of the most chaotic mass school shooting this nation has ever seen.

Aunt Catherine and my mom are speeding toward me and trying to hold it together, but they are both crying and saying to each other, "Not Kacey. How can it be Kacey? Not after the year she's had!" Their hearts are racing nearly as fast as the car carrying them to the crime scene. What will they see? Breath doesn't come naturally to either of them.

On Peakview, they are met by mass chaos, a web of cars and ambulances and police vehicles. Helicopters are already flying high above, everyone scrambling to figure out what is happening. My parents are only thinking of me.

Aunt Catherine pulls up and stops the car as an ambulance narrowly squeezes by, sirens blaring. My mom throws the door open and starts running down the sidewalk toward what looks like a triage area set up in the cul-de-sac ahead. She sees a middle-aged man walking toward her carrying a cell phone and he looks horrified. She knows it's him.

"Is she okay?" she asks breathlessly.

"She looks like she's been hit by a grenade," he says. He doesn't even have to mention my name. They just know. And God just knew how to bring them together.

My mom asks where I am, and he says, "She was in that ambulance that just left and they're heading to St Anthony's Hospital." My dad pulls into the crowded street and sees the ambulance leaving, noticing my Aunt Catherine's car parked nearby. He spots my mom. She jumps into his car; they turn the vehicle around quickly and begin driving north on Wadsworth. Aunt Catherine follows them in her car.

My mom is hysterical. After hearing the report from my mom, my dad thinks they have lost me. "How could she survive being hit with a grenade?" But he is so laser focused on getting them to the hospital that he keeps his emotions at bay. "You need to be prepared to lose her," he tells my mom. He keeps thinking to himself, "This cannot be happening. Not to my Kacey. This cannot be happening."

Their first actual conversation in the car is the strangest one of my dad's life. They are debating about stopping at the school to pick up Britney and Brett in case there is an opportunity to say goodbye to their sister. The school is right on the way. Do they waste the time?

Instead, they pull over. Aunt Catherine stops her car behind them. She runs up to the driver's side window and my dad tells her to go to the school to get the kids. They will meet them at the hospital. At this point, emergency vehicles are jamming Wadsworth Boulevard; onlookers whose cars had been pushed to the side of the road are trying to grasp what is happening. They will know soon enough. The whole world will know.

At Front Range Christian School, my sister Britney goes to the office to call my parents and let them know that their school is on lockdown, along with every other school in the area. She can't get in touch with either of them, so instead dials our dad's receptionist, Janet. She tells Britney that there are bombs in her sister's school and that our dad is on the way to help her. The first thing Britney thinks is "Oh my word, my sister's fallen in with troubled kids again, and she's gotten herself bombed."

She drops the phone and starts to cry. Brett is walking in from a football game on the playground and sees her crying in the office.

When Britney picks up the phone again, Janet asks if she wants to be retrieved from school. Without answering, Britney flees to Brett's classroom. He already knows something is terribly wrong. He thinks one of our horses has died. Britney is sobbing. Since the church and the school use the same building, Aunt Catherine and our newly informed and deeply concerned pastor then walk through the doors and corral my siblings. My aunt says something has happened to me, and some boys have gone into my school with shotguns and grenades. She tells them that I've been wounded and that she has to get them to the hospital to potentially say goodbye to me.

My brother goes from being a normal eleven-year-old, playing hockey and football, to what he describes as feeling like DefCon10. "I'm not sure I can breathe, like when you're about to drop on a roller coaster and your stomach twists. The hair on the back of my neck is standing up." Aunt Catherine whisks them away in her car.

Aunt Catherine tells them to be strong for me, so they are not to cry. My siblings feel that it takes forever to get to the hospital, even though in reality it only takes twenty minutes. Brett notices that every minute is distinct and different from the last. Britney is holding her breath, not knowing if I am going to live or die. My little brother is massaging a stress ball he finds in the back seat.

Continuing north on Wadsworth, my parents are preparing to lose me. They are discussing things they could not have dreamed up, repeatedly asking each other how a person can get hit by a grenade and survive. My mom is crying. My dad is strangely calm. Their lives were normal just thirty minutes ago.

At the intersection of Wadsworth Blvd and Sixth Avenue, my mom's cell phone rings. It is a call neither of my parents is expecting. I'm in an ambulance, bleeding to death, and I have the presence of mind to remember to give my mom's cell phone number to the paramedics. I feel sort of guilty about it, but I'm just not ready to talk to them yet. I have to survive first.

The paramedic says, "Hi, I'm in an ambulance with your daughter."

Desperate for answers, my mom asks in one long breath, "Is she okay? Can I talk to her? Where are you going?"

"She's been hurt badly, but we think she's going to live. You're going to St Anthony's, right?" he asks.

"Yes, we're on our way," my mom says and then hangs up the phone, incredulous.

My parents don't know how to respond to the phone call. They are trying to reconcile the first description given to them by the man who had been with me in triage with the information the paramedic just communicated. It's a ping-pong of emotions and they are completely raw. There is no control to be had here. The world is spinning on its axis, and they both feel dizzy.

My dad continues toward the hospital, focused on how to solve this unsolvable problem, wondering what he is about to see in the emergency room. My mom is crying in the seat beside him, sure that the man who saw me in triage is more correct in his description of my injuries. She is totally convinced I'm not going to survive. My dad is making an attempt to apply rational thought to a totally irrational situation. His foot pushes harder on the accelerator.

In the last five minutes of the drive, my mom calls her dear friend, Debbie Olson, to ask their small Bible study group to start praying. Then she calls her elderly dad in Michigan and a fellow parent from the kids' school to let them know what is going on. My dad swerves into the hospital parking lot and finds a space quickly. They run to the entrance of the emergency room not knowing what they will find inside. My siblings and Aunt Catherine are ten minutes behind them.

The glass doors part to the ER and my parents rush up to the front desk. They make it known they want to see me immediately. They are told they can't see me, that the staff is busy doing everything they can to stabilize me. My dad makes it very clear that they will be seeing their daughter. NOW.

I am in X-ray when my family arrives at St Anthony's Hospital. While they are standing in the hallway, they catch a glimpse of me from a distance as I roll by on a gurney. I am wrapped in white blankets with my head propped on a pillow, tilted to the left a bit, with my feet turned to the right. I see my parents walk into the room where doctors and nurses are busily working on me. Dad steps in first, followed by Mom. Careful not to frighten me and doing his best to mask the panic he feels, Dad calmly asks, "Kaccy, what happened?"

"Daddy, I got shot." It's all I can say. My very first tears start falling. Somehow in this moment I feel guilty that my parents have to see me this way; I know the excruciating pain it will cause them.

My parents notice that my blue jeans are soaked in blood. My blonde hair has been colored a bright red and I'm lying in a pool of the same color. They see the hole in my shoulder and the hole in my right hand. My mom's eye is drawn to a piece of my blonde hair running through the middle of the hole in my hand, threaded there by a powerful blast. My hands had been right next to my head, plugging my ears when I was shot. They wonder about the burn marks across my throat.

I feel every poke and prod that the staff make and can tell when they insert a catheter to relieve my bladder. I am very aware. I want to talk.

"Daddy, did you see the hole?"

Using my eyes, I direct their gaze toward the back of my right shoulder. They see a huge hole with hair, blood, tissue, and bones peeking out of it. My mom is processing everything analytically. She knows this is not good, that I am in critical condition, and that somebody should be getting me into surgery. My shoulder bones are shattered, and there is no real structure remaining to support my right arm. My dad notices this right away, but he asks about something else first.

"Kacey, what happened to your hand?"

"I was plugging my ears," I whisper.

He asks if I can control my hand, and I move it ever so slowly. It is a baby step toward hope for them. With every word I utter, every movement I make, my parents' ability to feel hopeful increases.

Shotgun slugs are built with cotton and plastic, and my mom sees some of that material in the exit wound on the front of my shoulder. A shotgun slug has torn through her seventeen-year-old daughter's body on a regular Tuesday, she thinks to herself, when she should have been at home eating cookies.

My younger siblings are eventually allowed into the room. There is now a big red patch of gauze on my shoulder and the red graze marks on my throat have become more pronounced. Brett wonders if I am going to suffocate from the tightening in my throat I have just described, and the eerie silence begins to scare him. He turns off his emotions, going into "fight" mode. He wants to switch places with me.

I'm lying there, shaking. My sister Britney strokes my hair and her hands get coated in blood. I ask her not to touch me, telling her that everything hurts. My dad points out the entry and exit wounds to my brother and sister. Brett thinks the exit wound on my chest looks like a volcanic cone of blood. He is hopeful I will survive though, because he has seen me communicate a little; at least he recognizes a small part of me. Britney seems to think I have already been stitched with fishing line, when instead it is a full view of my muscles and tendons. Nothing about the images of this day is age-appropriate.

Britney and Brett are escorted back to the waiting room as a policeman approaches me and begins to fire off a myriad of questions. It's obvious I am not doing well; even a thirteen-year-old and an eleven-year-old can see that. As Britney exits the room, she hears me tell the police officer, in a small voice, that I sort of got pushed out of the library. It felt like running through the narrow neck of a bottle. But he wants to know the whole story because the police don't yet know if the shooters are dead. Authorities only understand that it is still an active shooter situation. He wants to know what I saw, what guns were used, and I manage to tell him I saw two barrels when I looked back over my shoulder right before I was shot.

My Uncle Doug arrives as all this is unfolding—Aunt Catherine's husband and my dad's brother. He stands at the back wall like a statue, queasy at the unbelievable sight he is observing: his niece laying on a gurney with gaping wounds. My mom is standing there taking in the absurdity of the moment. She knows I should be in surgery. Saving my life should be considered first. Investigations should at least wait until the bleeding has stopped; my family quickly gets furious with the policeman.

Friends are beginning to fill the waiting room; the TV is blaring. Everyone starts to get a picture of what is happening at Columbine, though many pieces of the puzzle are still waiting to be found. There is no real understanding of motive, intent, or damage. Of gravest concern is the issue of additional shooters still on the loose. No one has a frame of reference for this event, as it has never happened like this before. It is impossible to know at this point how many people are involved.

Britney sits in the waiting room and asks God to let her keep her sister, and even if He allows her arm to be cut off, to please just keep her sister here. "God, if you could save my sister's arm, that would be good, too," she prays quietly.

Our family friend, Marshall Olson, tells my siblings to start calling people. They call everyone we know, telling them to come to St Anthony's to sit with the family during my surgery. It's then that Brett remembers our brother, Brian, has not heard the news. He is a junior at the University of Kentucky in Lexington studying business with hopes of going to law school.

There is no TV on at Brian's house, and he has just finished registering for his senior year earlier that morning. He's hanging out at his house with his roommate who is also his debate coach, and they are getting ready to strategize about upcoming debate matches. The phone rings.

"Brian, it's Brett. Kacey's been shot."

"What? What? Shut up, Brett. Shut up. I don't believe you." He's only eleven, after all.

"No, Brian. Turn on the news. I'm not kidding. Kacey's been shot at Columbine. I think she's going to live but her arm might get cut off," he says.

Brian does not take him seriously, but goes to his bedroom and closes the door, the phone jammed against his jaw. His roommate is watching him and moves toward the TV as Brian leaves the room.

He keeps asking Brett if I'm going to be okay. Brett just tells him to get on the next flight out. Realizing there is truth to what he is saying, Brian begins to cry uncontrollably, feeling helpless 1,300 miles away. He hears the TV confirm his fears in the other room. After hanging up the phone, Brian and his roommate watch in horror as news outlets repeatedly display Columbine students running out of the school to face police with their guns drawn.

Brian's life flashes before him, his whole childhood, even his high school debate finals that had been at Columbine. He can't make any sense out of it and his whole body begins to tremble. He reaches out to his best friend, Sean, in Boulder, who knows him well, and he proves to be deeply consoling. After three to four hours of helplessly watching the footage on the TV, and desperately wanting to be with his family, he collapses in exhaustion.

Back in Denver, there is concern that my brachial artery has been hit, and further tests are needed to confirm *the condition of my lungs before they can take me to the operating room. My dad demands to go back with me, but the staff only allows him to observe the tests through a window. I see my dad standing there helplessly, wanting to protect me, and it is the last thing I remember about the day. My mom goes to the waiting room and finds Spike sobbing in a chair; my friend is devastated that she never called to tell me she was sick at home and didn't plan to go to school. My mom is doing her best to calm Spike down. There are now forty people quietly milling in the special waiting room they have provided for my family.*

On the way back to the pre-op waiting area, my dad calls his mother in Indiana and there is no answer. He does not leave a message. He then calls the oldest of his nine siblings, Sandra. When she answers, she can immediately tell something is terribly wrong from the sound of my dad's voice. She screams into the phone, "Greg, Greg, what is wrong, what is wrong? Greg, Greg . . . " He hangs up on her, his nerves sawed off, not wanting to handle her emotions in the moment. Thirty seconds later, he calls her back and asks if she is ready to talk. There is no time for outbursts today, not in his mind. There is a life to be saved! My dad tells his sister to track down their mother. My parents, family, and friends are assembling a mighty army of prayer warriors all over the country.

Although I'm heavily medicated at this point, the St. Anthony's Hospital staff wheels me by my family on our way to the OR for a brief goodbye. No one knows for sure if I will come out of surgery. I've lost so much blood. My mom looks down and sees my left-hand exit wound for the first time. It is the moment that my siblings and parents finally break down and cry. My mom is sure that I am at a critical point for blood loss, and they all watch me disappear behind closed doors with the staff. My family is in utter disbelief.

My loved ones hunker down in the waiting room, knit tightly together in circles of prayer and consolation. A man no one in the room recognizes sits down and tries to talk to my sister and my dad. My dad's protective radar is always up, but ever more so on this day, and he quickly tells the man to leave. He instructs my siblings to avoid speaking with anyone they do not know; the media is in disguise, and they are hungry for the inside scoop. There will be more reporters on the prowl before night's end.

I survive the first surgery. It has taken the surgeons three or four hours just to tag my tissues, debride my wounds, and assess the damage. Once I'm safely in recovery, my parents and the surgeons meet in the hallway to discuss my condition. My anxious parents are searching their faces for any kind of clue; the doctors assure them that I will most likely survive. The surgeons describe having to remove seventy-three pieces of bone and lead from my wounds. A fixator is placed on my shoulder to hold my arm in place because all the supporting bone structure is damaged; they have no idea how to repair it.

My mom is unable to continue listening to the report after she hears I will survive, and relief floods her body for the first time all day. My dad believed I would live after hearing the paramedics' assessment on the way to the hospital. But, paying careful attention to the doctors' specific descriptions of my injuries still leaves him feeling shocked. As he fights through his emotions, he knows other families will be getting far more terrible news today. It appears that regardless of my catastrophic injuries, my family will get to keep me. But the day is saturated in sadness.

The surgeons give my mom and dad the graphic pictures they have taken during the surgery to document the damages. After announcing to the relieved crowd in the waiting room that I will survive this day, my parents share the photos with them. Some look at the photos, and some do not. They are not easy pictures to look at.

My family is ushered back to see me in the ICU about an hour later. Three other Columbine victims fill the beds next to mine; we all will be counted on the list of survivors. Brett notices a boy with a large bandage wrapped around his head; a boy who actually leapt out of the library windows after being shot in the head. It is in that moment that he understands the severity of the whole situation.

Finally, at 8:00 p.m., my mom drives herself home and my siblings go with our family's dear friends, Bob and Debbie Olson. Britney and Brett feel they have had to be strong for everyone all day, but when they arrive at the Olson's home, they collapse into bed with our friends' children who do their best to console them.

Britney is numb; Brett falls asleep mulling over the notion that every moment of this day feels like a day unto itself. Days and days and days that are sure to haunt his dreams. Brian is anxiously waiting for his flight home from Kentucky, fully funded by United Airlines, a gift they have given to all my extended family. Everyone is reassured they will see me alive, but it does not make any of them feel better.

The ICU becomes my new home, and I find rest there in the haze of heavy painkillers, sheer exhaustion, and my dad's protective presence. At 10:00 p.m., he watches me fall asleep, my rearranged arm propped on a huge white pillow in the bed. He finally reclines in a big brown chair next to me and falls into a fitful sleep. He wakes quickly when he hears me stirring a few hours later.

"Daddy, are you here?" I ask quietly. I can't see him from my bed.

"Of course, honey, I'm here," he responds.

"Daddy, I really thought I was going to be okay. I pulled the chair in front of me."

My father begins to weep quietly as I drift back into my drug-induced slumber, finally free from the searing pain.

Hours later, I wake again.

"Daddy, are you here?" I whisper.

"Yes, honey. I'm here."

"Daddy, the gun had two barrels." And then I'm right back to sleep.

He watches me in the quiet, his oldest daughter fighting for her life after staring down two gun barrels through the wide gaps in a simple chair, a sure Hand on her back that he doesn't even know about yet. And here I am, fully alive, breathing on my own, telling him things he never could have imagined he would be hearing tonight after saying goodbye at the breakfast table this morning. He will remember this sacred night with incredible clarity; his private agony intertwined with hope. The relative quiet in the ICU gives him the time he needs to process his shock, and he settles back into his chair, feeling God's comforting presence permeating the room.

Many years down the road, my dad will think that the whole difficult year before today was actually worse. My departure from all my parents had ever known to be true about me was still so absolutely heart-wrenching to him. He will realize that I needed the helpful support mechanisms and the foundation of unwavering faith I gained in those difficult months to help me live out my "new normal." Perhaps God allowed the writing of some very painful pages in my life story to serve all that will come after Columbine. Dad will believe I was ready, even prepared, to sit under the table and take that shotgun blast. He can't imagine "Lacey Kacey" cowering in the library. No. The new Kacey greeted that experience with steel already in her bones.

Twenty miles away, my mother is lying quietly in my parents' bed in our empty home—a welcome retreat after the chaos of the day. Unable to sleep, she remembers that in February or March, she had watched an episode of The X Files. Tea Leoni had been shot in the shoulder while holding the hand of a character that was, for whatever reason, unable to die. In the end, he transferred Tea's injuries to himself and died in her place. It disturbed my mother so much that she called my dad at work that day.

"I'm worried I am being warned that something bad is going to happen to someone in our family, Greg."

She watched the show right on the heels of the troubling year I had endured, so it was not a strange thing to say at the time. My dad told her that he trusted her instincts, and they both began to pray about it. Lying in bed on the night of the shootings at Columbine, my mom realizes that she and my dad were oddly prepared for the phone call that came this morning. This brings my mother some sense of comfort before she eventually drifts into a fitful sleep.

My family will set up camp in the hospital for the next two weeks, a fortress of sorts to protect us from the swarming media, and "normal" will not return to us for a very long time. Will I have to face the world as an amputee? Can I start the healing process before my body is restored? Will I ever mount my horse again?

There is someone in Denver who can answer these questions, and he has already been consulted on my case, though we don't know that yet. He is a master at using tissue donations, a surgical innovator and visionary in every way, a man filled with endless passion for his hurting patients. Our upcoming introduction in the ICU will alter the course of both of our lives, plus thousands more. We are about to put into motion something that has a much broader scope than just the repair of my broken body. It will become clear that what was first intended for evil will instead be used for a greater good.

CHAPTER 5

HEROES

Heroes are born every day. Some heroes are genetically predisposed to greatness, I suppose, blessed with a rich family history of bravery and selflessness. Others are ripped out of their regular lives and thrown into heroic duties in a matter of seconds, revealing their true character in the process. Many others get to make calculated and thoughtful steps toward heroic acts. Shakespeare famously wrote, "Some are born great, some achieve greatness, and some have greatness thrust upon them." It has been my privilege to watch many kinds of heroes grace the path of my life.

I saw a spirit of heroism rise up from what appeared to be regular teenagers in the Columbine library, students who helped each other escape with little to no thought about their own personal safety. Other students used their clothing to soak up the blood from the wounds of their classmates outside of the school building. Most teachers I know qualify for heroism simply by showing up to work every day, year after year, selflessly sharing their talents for the sake of education and the privilege of helping to shape the lives of the next generation. But some of the men and women working at Columbine acted as physical barriers for their students in a bloodbath for which they had no training, going above and beyond the confines of their job descriptions. After teaching and coaching at Columbine for twenty-five years, Dave Sanders was shot in the hallway while trying to help his students escape the building. After retreating to a classroom with their bleeding teacher, some of his students put a sign in a window that read, "1 bleeding to death!" When help finally arrived, it was too late. But the heroism he demonstrated acting as a shield for his students has never been forgotten. Teachers battle for their students through often insurmountable odds; they are heroes in every sense of the word.

I met another hero, however, who further clarified for me what it means to be truly courageous. It is an emptying of oneself for the greater good, a laying down of reputation or status, to be used in a remarkable way for the benefit of mankind.

Dr. Ross Wilkins was born to a beautiful, kind mother and a brilliant father. He knew at an early age that he was going to be a physician, living and working in his beloved state of Colorado. A circuitous route awaited him, however. Admitted to the University of Colorado in Boulder as a freshman, parties and nonscientific courses like philosophy and religion trumped any interest in the competitive premed curriculum. He had a good time and built quite the social reputation. Not the reputation, however, that medical schools were looking for. After he met his wife, Jan, he got serious in his last two years at school, but it wasn't enough. He graduated with a BS in Molecular, Cellular, and Developmental Biology, but had not been accepted by any medical schools.

He decided to focus on a different course; he moved to Detroit with his new bride and worked as an electron microscopist as he completed his course work in human physiology at Wayne State University Medical School. Establishing his credentials through his research and course work, he was admitted to medical school there in 1974. These were difficult times; his mother was diagnosed with a serious head-and-neck cancer, he was completing his master's research and thesis, and his father's alcoholism became a major issue. Despite these obstacles, the educational opportunities at the old Detroit General Hospital were surreal. Because of short staffing and huge patient volumes, medical students were given responsibilities far beyond those normally assigned to students. Dr. Wilkins thrived in that environment, and it confirmed his love of the physician's life.

But he was anxious to return to Colorado, so he sought and obtained a surgical residency at University Hospital in

Denver working under Dr. Tom Starzl on the kidney and liver transplant service. In those early days of fast-paced and daring transplant surgery, he regularly spent six out of seven nights on the floor of the hospital, obsessed with his work. Blessed with a young wife and a son waiting to be born, the pressures on his young family were intense. Two nurses pulled him aside one night in his exhaustion and advised him to leave transplant surgery behind; his obsession was ruining his family and transforming him into someone they no longer recognized. He had lost all perspective amid the wild pace, constant adrenaline, and extraordinary hours of cutting-edge surgery. They asked him to consider using his skill set in orthopedics. He listened to those women that night on the hospital floor, and thousands of people are glad he did.

Dr. Wilkins switched his residency to orthopedic surgery in 1979. He worked with a mentor, Dr. James Miles, who challenged him on many levels. When working with children with bone cancer (most of whom died in those days), Dr. Miles, with tears in his eyes, said, "Ross, it is your job to fix this." The heavy emotional nature of the job took its toll, as many of his patients were the ages of his young children at home. Pediatric patients with bone cancer would undergo an immediate amputation and often die within months. He decided to make this his life's work; he took a fellowship at the Mayo Clinic in Orthopedic Oncology where he learned a new approach to these difficult problems, an integrated approach involving many medical and surgical specialists. This team assured the best care possible for patients with lives and limbs in jeopardy. Dr. Wilkins worked in establishing the Mayo Clinic Bone Bank to preserve donor bones to be transplanted in replacement of damaged or cancerous bones, and thereby prevent amputations.

Dr. Wilkins returned to Denver to teach at the University of Colorado and established a specialty practice in "limb preservation," which involved patients with limbs in jeopardy from cancer, infection, or trauma. He learned that timing is everything. In those years, he intuitively gathered techniques and tools from his colleagues that could not be learned in a textbook. He began to catch the vision for where all his experiences were leading him. In 1986, he and Dr. Tom Arganese founded the Institute for Limb Preservation, a unique team of specialists that was assembled to cooperatively and prospectively evaluate patients with limbs in jeopardy. During this same time, the Limb Preservation Foundation was established to fund patient assistance programs, scholarships, and pivotal research.

Over the years, the multidisciplinary approach to this effort developed as a collaborative effort, a rare thing in the fast-paced world of specialty surgery. There would be no personal agenda for power or status but instead consistent collaboration toward the end goal of restoring patients to wholeness. As a long-term patient, I came to benefit enormously from that approach.

Dr. Wilkins has always been passionate about what he does. It is a physically demanding job and emotionally very difficult. There are great successes, but patients who die of cancer and undergo unnecessary amputations are still hard on the soul. Throughout the early years of his career and to this day, his wife, Jan, has enabled him to follow his dreams, working hard to manage daily concerns so he can concentrate on the pressing matters at hand; her unwavering support has been invaluable to his success.

A few years down the road, the protocol developed in cooperation with the Colorado State University Animal Cancer Center would have the highest limb preservation and patient survival of any published study for children with bone cancer. With a strong team of specialists working together, Dr. Wilkins now feels he can continue advancements into the future; the Limb Preservation Foundation's research with stem cells and limb preservation is adding even more information to save more limbs and lives. Dr. Wilkins is very passionate about the family of patients, doctors, nurses, and volunteers that have sacrificed to make this unique system successful. In the future, the goal is to use this system as a model for additional specialties in other geographic areas.

On April 20, 1999, Dr. Wilkins was in the clinic across the street from Presbyterian/St. Luke's Hospital when he received phone calls about an arm and a leg on two different Columbine shooting patients.

He was in disbelief. This wasn't Chicago or Detroit. "How could this happen here?"

On April 21, a team of doctors at St. Anthony's hospital called Dr. Wilkins specifically about my case. Dr. Mitch Seeman—the head of trauma at St. Anthony's—told him about the extensive damage to my shoulder, arm, and hand; they had never seen anything like it before. They wanted to know his opinion and what might be possible.

My X-ray revealed total destruction of my shoulder bone and parts of my hand. Thankfully, the plumbing in my arm could be fixed relatively easily and wasn't the problem. The real miracle was that I sustained no nerve or neurovascular damage with the extent of my injuries.

Based on the information he had been given prior to examining me, Dr. Wilkins believed there were four possibilities:

1. Amputation: no function, phantom pain, difficult to wear prosthetic arm without some shoulder in place;
2. Leaving the flail arm attached: no shoulder function, eventual additional nerve damage;
3. Titanium replacement with artificial joint and bone: no active function of shoulder joint, no stability; or
4. Bone joint transplant: stable shoulder joint with some active function, no further nerve damage

In many limb-salvage surgeries, cancerous bone is removed carefully with no damage to the surrounding healthy parts. In contrast, the X-ray of my shoulder and arm looked like a bomb had gone off; the bones looked like dust particles in the images. I also had a four-inch-wide hole in the back of my shoulder that was missing muscle, skin, and tissue. Dr. Wilkins was not sure what to do because bone joint transplantation had never been attempted before on a trauma patient. His only experience was in oncology cases where the bone was transplanted into a very controlled environment. My shoulder and arm were anything but that; a chaotic mess of damaged bones, muscles, and tendons.

On April 22, Dr. Wilkins parked his car and navigated through throngs of security and frenzied media at the entrance to St. Anthony's Hospital. Because my parents had not yet chosen to release my name to the media, Dr. Wilkins had to describe my injuries to the front desk before being granted permission to enter the ICU. It took him several minutes to pass through hallways crammed with officials, family members, and staff. It became immediately apparent that my case wasn't going to be like any other he had been assigned.

He approached my door. Unbeknown to either of us, our introduction would change the course of both of our lives. He saw me lying there on the hospital bed, limp and sedated; the room was full of distraught family members and hospital staff. He took a deep breath and entered. The air was thick with tension.

Dr. Wilkins greeted us by shaking everyone's hand. Brian had just arrived from his long journey from Kentucky, jarred by his first look at me sleeping in my hospital bed with all my bandages; he felt especially appreciative of Dr. Wilkins's genuine warmth. Doctor after doctor had shown up to address my case in the two previous days, but each one had begrudgingly departed, determining my injuries were outside of their skill sets. When he arrived, my family was still wondering what medical miracle might eventually show up, and at this point, they wondered if it would ever show up at all.

My parents were scared for me, exhausted, frustrated with the lack of hopeful solutions to date, and running out of time to decide on an amputation or other potentially life-changing choices for their seventeen-year-old daughter. Dr. Wilkins knew he needed to handle the intensity of frustration, fear, and exhaustion that was apparent in my parents with great care. So, after performing an initial exam on my shoulder, he simply sat down. It was a posture he had used in the past that proved to be successful in highly tense situations, and this was clearly going to be an uneasy conversation. He paused for a moment, commanding silence in the room, and said with some authority, "Our biggest concern here is to prevent infection. But these are the four options as I see them." My medical team and family quietly listened to him as he walked them through each of the four possibilities for my shoulder, arm, and hand, everyone quickly realizing that he stood out above the rest as a true pioneer.

The rotator cuff tendons, most of my shoulder bone structure and the top six inches of my upper arm bone (humerus) were gone. Even though my shoulder and arm were the priority, it was clear my hand would need attention as well. My body was already reabsorbing the remaining damaged tissues. Placing a metal rod inside of me would not allow my traumatized tissues to heal to it, and that did not appear to be a viable option to anyone. Instead, Dr. Wilkins suggested replacing the lost bones in my arm and hand with allografts (donated human cadaver bone). While my body could potentially recognize them as dead tissue instead of foreign objects, he believed there was a good chance that my body would not reject them. Ideally, my tendons would heal to the donated bone in a biologic replacement, an unfolding mystery of modern medicine that would ultimately change the structure of my body, my recovery, and therefore, the trajectory of my life.

My tendons were beginning to shrink back with every passing hour, so each day that went by increased my risk that what was left of them would not successfully adhere to the donor bone. Time was of the essence. Dr. Wilkins felt hopeful about the transplantation, but did not think I would regain full functionality. "It's not ever going to be as good as the original equipment," he told my eager family, "but I think it gives her the best shot." His goal was to try to get me back to somewhat normal usage of my right shoulder. He had seen enough to know that people beat the odds and achieved great things postoperatively.

In his opinion, though, the patient must have ears to hear and eyes to see the vision. He knew right off the bat that my family was going to help me meet the challenge head on. Although my parents had lingering doubts about the risks, everyone agreed that a bone joint transplant seemed to be the smartest option.

All the surgeons agreed that the allograft surgery should be delayed until I was cleared from the risk of infection. I also had blood transfusions to replace the blood I had lost, and those procedures mixed with the heavy painkillers were giving me blinding migraine headaches.

During my time in the hospital, many cards, gifts, books, posters, plants, and flowers began to fill the ICU, cramming the nurses' station and every flat surface in sight. Additionally, the front rooms of our family home were filling with so many gifts that friends began to take copious notes about them so that we could send thank you notes at a later date. Thousands of cards arrived from around the world, full of messages of shock, sorrow, and promises of prayer. To this day Brett is repulsed by the smell of cut flowers; they make him sick to his stomach.

Columbine most certainly changed the landscape of our history, as well as put a face on school violence. As our nation mourned together, the gifts I received stood in my parents' living room as a monument of the solidarity the world was feeling about the atrocities. For the weeks and months after I returned home, I received a steady stream of beautiful bouquets of flowers and balloons, and even a large piece of art lovingly painted by a man at a homeless rescue mission. It featured a young girl lying on a bed with Jesus reaching down and touching her head; the notes of encouragement from all the people living at the shelter at the time really touched my heart. Most upsetting to me were the cards signed by entire classrooms of elementary school children. It bothered me that they knew what happened to me, but I was blessed by their care and concern. As recipients of such a giant outpouring of support, my family marveled over the incredible gestures of compassion and generosity.

The world initially knew me as the shoulder victim, or "Female, 17 years old", and each day the hospital staff updated my condition to the media. I stayed at "critical" for the first two days, and then moved down to "serious" for most of my hospital stay. On the second day, I unexpectedly saw an update on the television in the ICU. They aired a generic silhouette and it said, "Female, 17 years old, critical condition." It scared me to death. Was I in critical condition? It took my parents a while to console me, as they had worked so hard to keep anything negative out of my room to keep my attention and energy focused on healing. On the third day after the shooting, my parents finally released my name to the media.

I barely ate anything in the hospital, mostly just tiny bowls of Fruit Loops and an occasional apple. Though protein is necessary for proper healing, my poor appetite and calorie intake would prove problematic for many months in the future; everyone was worried I was going to be permanently emaciated. My wounds were not just physical in nature.

The media barrage was a constant nuisance, but my family was carefully sheltered from the circus that had gathered directly outside of the hospital. One reporter tried to pay a family friend to slip a camera up to the ICU to get some pictures. His response was quite colorful! All the hospital security, my family, and our friends were fiercely protective of me; the hospital staff did a great job of building up a strong barrier around all of us. It was a daily battle.

The police were continually trying to piece together what had actually happened inside the library. My parents witnessed a number of officers break down in tears over what had happened to me and the other students. Some developed PTSD from the massacre at Columbine and retired or moved on from law enforcement. It's easy to forget that these men and women—whose careers hinged on heroism—were human; many of them were parents. The scenes they witnessed at Columbine and then had to recreate and analyze proved devastating.

Two days after my first surgery, my second operation further cleaned out my wounds to guard against any dreaded infection. Swollen from the fluids they had pumped through me during the surgery and coming out of the fog of anesthesia only a few hours into my recovery, I felt like I resembled the Michelin Man. I was not in a place to entertain visitors, and most certainly not cute boys or professional athletes on whom I had long-term crushes!

Some of our friends told the chaplain of the Colorado Avalanche hockey team that my favorite player was Peter Forsberg. Without any warning, he and seven other Avs players showed up in the ICU—THE Peter Forsberg!!!! It's amazing I didn't have a heart attack!

My parents were very excited to see the group walking down the hallway, knowing I would enjoy their visit. I was just alert enough after surgery to be giddy about my teenage crush standing next to my bed. When they came into my room, my increased heart rate set off all the alarms on my heart monitors. I even had the wild, drug-induced thought, "Sure, shoot me! If it makes all my dreams come true, off with my shoulder already!" I was only slightly disappointed that Peter left my room without asking me out.

The signed gear they brought me that day now decorates the walls of my parents' basement. Their visit really lifted the spirits of my siblings, especially my little brother whose whole life revolved around hockey. It was a dream come true for him. As a small eleven-year-old processing an otherworldly situation, he desperately needed the unexpected distraction. We all did.

After the players exited my room, Peter was leaning up against the wall in the hallway. As my mom began showing some of our friends the pictures of my wounds that were now hidden under heavy bandages, he accidentally took a peek. His face went white and my mom almost had to call the nurses. When my mom asked if he wanted to see any other pictures, in a low and shaky voice, he said, "Um, no, thank you." She was in hysterics later. Peter Forsberg, THE Peter Forsberg, had almost passed out right next to her! It would have been her fault, too. We all love that story.

The next Monday arrived; the team of surgeons, nurses, and staff were prepped and ready for my big surgery. All of Dr. Wilkins's transplantation surgeries were performed at Presbyterian/St. Luke's Medical Center (PSL), but because of the media frenzy at St. Anthony's, a plan was put into place to secretly transfer me. I hardly remember the transfer due to the cloud of painkillers, but riding in an ambulance again—albeit with my dad by my side—brought back a lot of the initial terror from April 20. I arrived safely and was admitted through a back entrance. A male nurse greeted my ambulance, sending me into a panic. I was unreasonably afraid of men; at St. Anthony's, I had requested that only female staff be allowed to care for me.

There was a theory circulating and being discussed on the various news channels that a third shooter existed. He was supposedly a friend of the killers, but chickened out of the mission once the boys got to the school to begin their shooting spree. The rumor was eventually dispelled, but I was convinced nearly every male I saw was the third shooter in disguise, ready to finish me off. I didn't even allow my youth pastor from church to visit me at the hospital. The feeling of being targeted by all violent people in the world remained with me for years.

Three nurses were assigned to me at PSL. The consistency they brought to my care was a huge part of my successful recovery process. Patty, Julie, and Denise worked around the clock to keep me comfortable and to provide the bedside support I so desperately needed. I remember those weeks in the hospital with tender affection. The devotion of the three women working on the sixth floor, heroes in their own right, would lead to some pretty remarkable developments in my near future.

I was given a private room as well as the use of the room next to mine so my family had a "home away from home." My dad spearheaded the private and spacious accommodations for us, knowing that I had to be protected from the crowd of people wanting to get to me. Dr. Wilkins was supportive of the plan; my healing would not be inhibited, not on his watch! His commitment to "whole person care" really became apparent as he led those initial decisions and helped us set up camp at PSL. Dr. Wilkins cared about more than just my physical well-being. It was obvious he was going to champion my case for the long haul, and his deep investment in my life and recovery is something that still brings me to tears today.

On Sunday, before my third surgery, my parents went to the public Columbine Memorial service at Clement Park for the thirteen victims who died in the shooting. I was left to face some quiet hours at the hospital for the first time without my safety nets. My blonde hair had been colored by blood for days; I knew I looked like a disaster but finally felt well enough to accept some help with my personal grooming. My sister and my horse trainer, Barbie, who had previously worked as a nurse, headed to the hospital. They washed my hair three times to get it clean and shiny again. Initially, I struggled a lot with feeling abnormal, but being clean made me feel more like a normal person; I felt sort of "cute" again. Barbie and Britney attended to little things each day after that: getting me comfortable in bed, adjusting my pillows for better arm support, providing drinks and snacks, and switching my TV channels. Every blessing helped me jump over the next big hurdle with more confidence. The little things truly do add up to some pretty big things in my book. I will forever be grateful for their selfless service during those scary and confusing days.

Searching tissue banks to find the right donor bone was surprisingly not difficult. Dr. Wilkins put in his request for a humeral cryopreserved allograft and another allograft for my hand. This request went to AlloSource, a tissue processing facility in suburban Denver. The bone they had "in the freezer" was a perfect match for my shoulder, and they had bones to match my hand as well. Dr. Wilkins was a cofounder of AlloSource. The nonprofit tissue processor receives donated tissues (bone, skin, tendons) from Organ Procurement Organizations, and their highly trained staff prepare the tissues for surgical use. AlloSource generously donated the bones for my limb-salvage procedure; I was unaware what an allograft meant at the time. But my parents understood that the bone used to save my arm was available because another family had lost their young daughter. It did not fall lightly on them that just a week prior they were mere minutes away from being in the same situation. Accepting a gift that came through such profound loss for another family added another layer of grief to my parents' aching hearts.

In a six-hour surgery late on Monday morning, April 26, 1999, Dr. Wilkins first took out all the remaining debris he could find in my shoulder and arm. At that point, he could see the rotator cuff tendons, part of which were thankfully still there. There was just enough supporting tissue remaining to make a successful repair. He and his team implanted the donor bone to what was left of my humerus, connecting the two pieces with plates and screws. However, there was quite a bit of missing muscle behind my shoulder, which he knew might limit my functionality, but there was no better choice. Dr. Tom Mordick, an elite hand surgeon, was selected by my family and Dr. Wilkins to perform my right hand repair during the same surgery. An additional allograft was put in my hand to replace what was lost. It was unclear at the time of surgery what function, if any, I would regain with my thumb. I was right-handed, so it was of special concern to my family.

It proved to be a major surgery indeed; it would take me a long while to recover from the magnitude of it. I had not left the safety of my bed since arriving at the hospital and I ate very little. I quietly watched hours of news coverage after my third surgery, and I felt so sad each time I missed another funeral of a shooting victim. Not being present for those events weighed heavily on me. It broke my heart as each person was laid to rest; I wanted to grieve in person with their families. That would come in time, but though I had no choice, missing the funerals is still one of my greatest regrets.

Twenty-four hours after surgery, I attempted to walk from my bed to the door and back to the bed again. I had not been out of the bed at all until that day. The next morning, I hobbled to the hallway and back. Baby steps toward recovery. The drugs had some interesting side effects. I kept telling my dad that the Dixie Chicks were playing loudly and asked him to make them stop because I had a headache. He made a joke that maybe all the new metal in my shoulder was picking up a radio station. His attempts to convince me of the reality of the relative quiet in the ICU did not stop me from griping about it.

I would not feel recovered for years, but that did not change my motivation. I wanted to jump out of bed and run down the hall with the strength of my old body, but deep down I knew that this journey through recovery was a marathon, not a sprint. My family stayed by my side day and night for the entire two-week stay in the hospital. My dad did not even entertain returning to work for three months. Security was in place 24/7, and my parents approved each and every visitor.

Dr. Wilkins did not expect me to have full range of motion. He did not know me very well yet, but by that point he had learned of my love for horses from spending time with my family. The huge poster of Moxie that my friends sent to decorate my hospital room was a sure giveaway. I missed my horse so much; the barn felt so far away.

I asked Dr. Wilkins shortly after the surgery, "When am I going to be able to ride again?" I needed something to look forward to and he enthusiastically wanted to help me achieve my goals. His focus on "whole person care" remained perfectly intact. He laid out the steps, and never told me the dreaded "never." Dr. Wilkins holds the belief that there is no point in saving arms and legs if people aren't allowed to use them again. Critics may say he should not have let me ride again because of the risk of falling and the need for more surgeries, but he maintained that letting me back out on my horse again was a good decision. Competitive athlete that I was, Dr. Wilkins realized that I was a motivated patient and would do what it took to get back to the World Show in a year.

The staff at PSL learned how much I loved Avalanche hockey, and since it was playoff season, they brought in a special TV for each playoff game, so I would not miss any of the action. I still had to pinch myself that eight of the players had been standing in my room at St. Anthony's less than a week before! Even though I never made it through watching an entire game due to the haze of painkillers, my Uncle Doug faithfully came to my room to cheer on our beloved Avalanche with me.

Each day at the hospital, my family would receive a list of celebrities who wanted to drop by and encourage me. Every person living in Denver is a Broncos fan, and if they aren't, they had better stay quiet about it! We loved our recent, two-time Super Bowl Champion Broncos in 1999, and some of them sacrificed their time to bolster my family during our darkest hours. Jason Elam and Mark Schlereth were both men of faith, and invited me to their Bible study as they stood to leave after their gracious visits. Jason even let me try on his Super Bowl ring. Even though I put it on my left hand, I was so weak I could not lift my left arm high enough to admire the ring. He was helpful to support my arm as I giggled from embarrassment.

Running back Terrell Davis stopped by to visit me as well; he was so huge, his frame took up the entire doorway of my room! I was definitely my typical, shy self around him. He was at the height of his career, and his large stature totally intimidated me. What an incredibly nice guy with a grin that lit up my entire room; there was more than one nurse swooning over him! Head coach Mike Shanahan and my dad had a good talk in the hallway one afternoon, too. His daughter shared many common equestrian experiences with me and they talked at length about it. His visit really encouraged my hurting dad, and my sports-obsessed brothers appreciated every casual chat they got to have with athletes as well. It helped to lift the heavy blanket of grief for a little while. Although hockey will always be my sport of choice, I will be a Broncos fan as long as I live!

One morning, the PSL media coordinator approached my parents and asked them if maybe I would like for the band NSYNC to visit. They were scheduled for a concert in Colorado Springs, and their managers had specifically asked the hospital if they could come for a few minutes to encourage me. Um, YES PLEASE.

Cue the glamour squad. After living in a hospital gown for over a week and enduring three major surgeries, it is safe to say I was not quite ready to have Justin Timberlake wrap his arms around me. No, no. Time for an overhaul, people! My friends washed and styled my hair, helped me put on a bit of makeup, and somehow dressed my mangled body in street clothes for the first time. When the band arrived, I was sitting in bed, feeling as pretty as I could, under the circumstances.

I could hear them coming before they approached my door, the buzz building throughout the hospital as their huge bodyguards led the way for them to pass through the halls of the sixth floor. It was standing room only that day in my suite, and I blushed as each band member greeted me and said such nice and affirming things. The icing on the cake was being serenaded with *(God Must Have Spent) A Little More Time on You!* To think that the week before I had just been a regular girl grooming her horse, doing homework, and working as a hostess at a steakhouse—for crying out loud, this was amazing! I had now survived a massive school shooting, three major surgeries, a hug from Peter Forsberg, and freaking NSYNC serenading me! For a few minutes, I almost forgot that I had been shot, which meant their visit was a giant success.

Glamorous moments aside, I had the huge task of learning to live with my newly disabled body before I could be released from the hospital. I increased the distance of my walks each day, mostly at a snail's pace, but it qualified as progress all the same. My exit from the hospital was planned for May 2, 1999. Although I was anxious to be in the comfort and quiet sanctuary of home, I was equally terrified to leave the heavy security provided for us at the hospital. The three nurses who so graciously cared for me during my stay had to join forces with Dr. Wilkins to convince me that my greatest healing would happen at home. It felt like I was standing on a ledge and about to take a flying leap into a dark abyss. Not helping matters was the removal of the catheter they had placed in me when I first arrived at the hospital. The torture of having to crawl out of bed to prove I could pee on my own was painful and humiliating. But it was one of the first glimpses into my loss of the independence I had known before the shooting; I would feel the pain of that for quite some time.

The morning of my homecoming still stands out as a marker of the contrast between my two very different lives: pre- and post-Columbine. My parents denied multiple requests for a family press conference as we prepared to leave. Their desire for privacy took precedence over a need to educate the public on my condition. After carefully placing me in a wheelchair on the sixth floor, surrounded by my parents and nurses, we started the quiet descent in the staff elevator.

A crowd of hungry reporters met me with their cameras rolling on the ground floor. Even though I had been warned, I was scared and rendered speechless in response to the barrage of questions fired at me without a real security guard at my side; I refused to answer even one question. Nothing can prepare someone for a moment like that. I watched as my Uncle Doug's smooth-riding Lexus was brought to the curb and I was gently placed inside. It was clearly the beginning of a brand-new life, punctuated by the sounds of the world screaming for my attention outside of the car windows.

My life had become a story I was quite sure I did not want to write, much less live, but nonetheless I had to find a way to do so. I left the hospital utterly terrified, as evidenced by the picture someone snapped of me that got splashed across the nation's newspapers. But the God who sees all things, knows all things, and has a greater story into which I've been drafted made it obvious that my new path would contribute to the greater good. He entrusted me with something extraordinary during those eight minutes in the Columbine library. The truth of that has been revealed . . . but this, of course, did not happen overnight.

CHAPTER 6

MY "NEW NORMAL"

No one remembers their infancy, but at the age of seventeen I got a bird's-eye view of what it was like to be a baby again: helpless, needy, fragile, dependent. A new life was beginning whether I liked it or not, and like a newborn, I needed all the help I could get to attempt a rebuilding of my life. Waves of grief washed over the new road and added to my anxiety. I no longer felt like the normal teenager I once was; I could not even dress or wash myself, and that was embarrassing. Being alone in a room was not an option, either; the tiniest disruptions and noises sent ripples of fear through my whole body. I needed to be tucked, once again, under the protective wings of my parents, and it got dark under there pretty quickly. In reality, that meant that my siblings had to experience some level of neglect again, too. I may have been home, but our family was still living in the smoky haze of the Columbine bomb. The air wouldn't clear for a long time, as hard as we tried to blow it far, far away.

My family members were now tasked with making me feel secure twenty-four hours a day, and it took an entire house full of people to get us through those first few foggy months. My parents spent their time focusing on my pain medication schedule, medical appointments, counseling sessions, and FBI interviews. It would often take fifteen minutes just to get me into a position on the couch that relieved a tiny bit of pain. Because I needed their attention full-time, extended family members continued to fly in to help care for my siblings, clean the house, prepare meals, and sort through the constant stream of gifts and cards. We were grateful, but there was virtually no privacy.

Hardest on my parents was attempting to ease all the fears I had brought home with me from the hospital. They had neither a framework nor any history from which to draw. They quickly learned that one of the only places I felt completely safe was at the barn. And, because my sister was still able to train, we made frequent trips to our trainers' facility in Parker. Nothing was more soothing to me than standing beside my horse, Moxie. The first time I walked up to him, he instinctually knew I was not okay. He very gently put his head down by my legs and nudged me with his nose. He then moved his nose up to check out the very large bandages up and down my right arm. The familiarity this strong, beautiful animal demonstrated helped me tremendously. He didn't judge me or ask any questions. I could just BE around him. Those day trips to the barn infused life back into my soul, slowly but surely.

One of the best parts of being at home was the chance to look through the thousands of cards and gifts that now occupied my parents' living and dining rooms. I had only imagined how the gifts would look when I was in the hospital; the real pile was astoundingly tall. A skyscraper of kindness, really. I could not believe how many people took time to reach out to my family; the generosity was completely overwhelming. There were notes from elementary school classrooms, family members I had never met, strangers from across the world, and even a few from concerned people living in jail. I did not want to throw one thing away; as I trudged through a long recovery, the gifts felt like life preservers floating around me. I was not alone, and I was not going to drown. Even today, my parents have a storage room in their basement dedicated to the love offerings we received so many years ago.

Most of my days were spent behind locked doors managing my pain and trying to figure out my new body. I had no use of my right arm or hand. I was learning to dress myself and tie my shoes with one hand and trying to write left-handed for the first time. Ponytails were tricky, and at seventeen, I cared about how my hair looked! Youth group friends made frequent visits to our home to play Uno with me. One boy even built me a custom cardholder, so it would be easier for me to play the game I loved.

There was a great concern growing between my parents and the professionals surrounding me about my ability to discipline my mind in those first few weeks; sliding back into the inky darkness of the library was easy to do, and that would prove a giant hurdle to my healing. The greatest inhibitor to my recovery by far was the mental struggle. I was put on mood-boosting medication to help fight depression, the strongest of sleep aids to help me rest, and heavy painkillers which were barely enough to stay on top of the bone-deep pain I was initially experiencing twenty-four hours a day. With my PTSD running rampant through my mind, the medications helped me move closer to my goal of complete healing.

God was faithful in helping me manage a few flashes of anger; it never took up permanent residence in my heart or mind. I never did ask, "Why me?" I knew why, really; I knew deep in my spirit. People often question that, but it's true. It was very clear that God had used that awful year before the shooting to prepare my faith and my strengths specifically for the event at Columbine and for my new story. I knew He would provide all I needed to somehow overcome this: whether I got to use my arm again or not. I was just anxious to get back to normal, however that might look. But I needed to know what was possible, not what was probable. Probable felt depressing and constricting, and I mostly kept my eyes locked on the prize of what was possible.

As the weeks of recovery floated by, and the prescription painkiller bottles were repeatedly refilled, it became clear that I was too medicated and weak to complete the schoolwork that a tutor faithfully brought to my home each week. All of the Columbine victims were given the option to accept the grades they had earned when the shooting happened; we were not required to finish the rest of the semester. Because I was a good student with excellent grades, I quickly chose this option. The rest of the student body was attending school at Chatfield High School now. Columbine and Chatfield had always had a healthy but intense rivalry. Nevertheless, Chatfield opened its doors to welcome the hurting Columbine population so they could finish the school year; it would be hard to find a better example of community support. Rival student bodies finished out the semester shoulder to shoulder, but I was happy to delay my return to a school setting.

Somewhere between appointments with doctors and therapists, days spent at the barn watching my peers' rigorous training, and the occasional ponytail meltdown in my bathroom, I had an intense interview with the FBI. The actual FBI—in MY home. This "new normal" felt so surreal every single day. The presence of official-looking staff in our home was deeply unsettling to me, but I wanted to contribute to their investigation, so I did my best to move past the intimidating situation and quickly got to work. The men and women needed to record everything I could remember, and I remembered A LOT. Before we got started, a kind agent gently reminded me that when people are in traumatic situations they have trouble grasping a sense of time and details. I think I shocked them when I recounted so many pieces of the story accurately; including the amount of time I spent in the library—down to the exact minute!

About halfway through our talk, they started to doubt the details I provided of the events in the library. They doubted my description of the gunman shooting me from behind. The agents told me that was not possible; exit wounds are larger than entrance wounds, and my wounds were just the opposite. I would soon get my chance to prove my version of the story, and believe me when I say I had a burr under my saddle about this detail. I knew exactly what happened.

After some long discussions, it was decided by a group of psychologists working with the injured victims and their families, as well as the families of the deceased, that all parties should be allowed to view the damaged school and library about a month after the shooting, before its final clean-up. It was supposed to be an opportunity for healing and closure for victims and their families, but the days leading up to the viewing gave me great anxiety. I wondered how this would aid my progress; it felt more like an uncertain slide backward. My parents, of course, wanted to see the room where all of this had happened to me, and I didn't begrudge them that. It was difficult for them to understand everything I was talking about without seeing it in person. Of great concern to everyone was how I would react to being in that room again. I was terrified to go, but in some way I was relieved to get the chance to physically reenact my story in the actual setting: I knew from which direction I had been shot. I wanted to prove the FBI agents wrong; they weren't going to change my story in the record books if I had anything to do with it.

The morning of the visit, my dad parks the car in the Columbine parking lot, the same lot in which I had perhaps escaped death by not going home for lunch on April 20. If I had walked to my Ford Explorer that day, I would have walked straight into the shooters when they began their spree in the parking lot. Thinking about that, my feet feel strangely heavy hitting the warm pavement as I slowly climb out of the car. It is May, and bright Colorado wildflowers greet us along the sidewalk up to the school, signs of life that will be a stark contrast to what lies inside. Clement Park nestles the Columbine building, and I keep thinking about the thirteen makeshift memorials constructed on the other side of the school in a quiet spot frequented by thousands of visitors. This once ordinary place will never be the same, earmarked as something grotesque forever. What should have been a day to set up the school for graduation is instead a formal and somber crime scene complete with a very visible police presence. It feels like accidentally sauntering into a shopping mall that has been turned into a funeral home, all the embalming procedures on display for public viewing. Everything feels inappropriate and weirdly out of context. No amount of counseling could have prepared my family for what they are about to see and smell and step over. I feel afraid; I want the sheriffs to go down the halls before us with their guns drawn, to make sure the coast is clear. I slowly walk behind them with my parents, with Brian and Britney right on my heels, peeking around each corner before entering the next hallway. I feel small and scared and more timid than I ever have in my life. Melted popsicles have left strange marks on the floor, and the colors make my sister cringe. Seeing the double doors to the library brings back searing memories of the day I nonchalantly wandered in with my gossip magazine in hand. I would never be that girl again. I miss her acutely in this moment.

It is a scene straight out of a horror movie, the overpowering smell of dried blood and gunpowder quickly apparent to all of us. The plastic that covers the broken windows rattles in the wind as we try to survey the room, and I keep thinking about the boy who fell out of one of the large windows with an injured leg and a bullet lodged in his brain. "At least he got out," I think to myself.

It is a cluttered mess, exactly as we had left it; gun powder stains, shattered pipe bomb remnants, broken computer screen glass, overthrown chairs, backpacks, books, and scattered evidence markers. Nothing has been cleaned up. My backpack is still leaning against the chair I had been sitting in to read. The large pool of my blood is still on the carpet under the computer desk where I was shot, and the chair that had been my shield is where I left it, the blood marking my exact spot on the floor. A small nick in the chair shows the path of the slug just before it hit my shoulder. I can't help but glance at the places I know some of my schoolmates were killed; remembering some of their final moments while standing in the exact spots they lost their lives is a little like standing at the funerals I never got to attend. I nearly choke on the heavy sorrow I feel.

After the initial shock of the environment wears off, I am all business. I reenact my version of the story for the officers and agents in attendance; I awkwardly kneel down, crouch, and then point with my left hand to show them how my memory of the shooting spree played out. My words articulate the crystal clarity of the scene in my mind; I have no doubt as I slowly recount every minute of the horror. As we prepare to leave, my parents look physically relieved to have been given the chance to gain visual understanding of everything I have been describing for a month. It finally makes sense to my family, the police, and the FBI agents, and no one questions me as we prepare to leave the room. My reenactment proves that I have been right all along. I was shot from behind, at close range.

For me, this is the very beginning of owning my story, of glimpsing the potential power in it. After a month of only being able to use words to describe my experience, I am finally able to act it out, allowing those who love me to see the bloodbath I have survived.

Standing back up on my feet as I pull myself up from that library floor, albeit bandaged and bruised, is such a moment of triumph. I survived the evil; for reasons unbeknown to me, I have survived. As I exit the library, I determine to find the beauty in the ashes of this experience if it is the last thing I ever do on this earth.

With the mental pictures, distinct smells, and the eerie silence etched in their minds, my family was now better equipped to understand how to walk with me as I trudged down the road toward healing. The scope of what they witnessed in the library swiftly rewrote their initial mental summaries of the event, however: it was far worse than they had ever imagined, and my siblings struggled with the overwhelming imagery for years. We were all very quiet on the ride home, and none of us felt like eating for the rest of the day. Never again would we bear witness to a scene so intimately horrific, and it was hard to know how to start processing it. God's presence stayed with all of us, though; a very real and anchoring peace in the midst of a storm for which the world had no reference points to offer us. We would just have to be patient with ourselves and with the professionals surrounding us.

For the next three months, I once again set up camp in my parents' bedroom, sleeping on my mattress that we laid on the floor. As the counselors predicted, my mind refused to turn off; I was always on guard for the subsequent attack I thought for sure was coming. I even accused Brian—who announced on a whim that he was coming home from college one day—that he must be coming home to kill all of us, much to his horror. It was not uncommon for me to make irrational pronouncements about what I perceived of the intentions of even those closest to me.

No amount of painkillers or sleeping pills could put me to sleep, and every night felt like Groundhog Day. Our routine was the same each evening; Dad would walk through the house next to me, showing me that every window was shut and every door was locked. And, sometimes, I would make him take me around a second time, just to be sure. Then, I would take my meds, hoping this was the night they would actually work and provide a respite from the anxiety. When the pills were not successful in knocking me out, I would sit in the TV room with Dad and watch *SportsCenter*. All. Night. Long. I could recall every stat from every sport. And, if Dad ever dozed off, I would quickly wake him up so he could keep his watch over me. Often, we would not make our way into our beds until 4:00 a.m., when our bodies finally surrendered to exhaustion.

For months, my dad stood like a soldier watching over our home. The nights I spent with my dad reflect the same loving devotion he showed me the year before the shooting, when I refused to speak with him, defiant and unstable. Only now, sitting next to him on the couch at night was the only place I felt safe in the world.

I wish I could say my healing progressed quickly, that I started to feel normal as the days passed. But so often, that just isn't how healing works. The waiting was slowly killing me. Shortly after the shooting, my dad noticed my attitude toward people growing increasingly rude, probably the result of a fuse cut short by bone-deep pain and a heavy dose of anxiety. On a visit to see Dr. Wilkins in his office in early June, I was in a particularly bad mood. After the exam and some talk about what came next, I casually asked his opinion about mounting my horse and returning to competitions. For some reason, I had it in my head that he said I could be back on my horse within a month of the shooting: what was the hold up, I wondered? Apparently, I had conjured that notion in one of my drug-induced, postsurgery hazes. But I demanded an explanation, and I wasn't nice about it. When Dr. Wilkins calmly explained that I was too frail, and the shoulder was still too precarious for serious exercise (not to mention my altered mental state), I pounced on him, "What?! You're a liar! You told me I could be back up on my horse in a month!" My tears fell unchecked, and I could see my dad's red face getting darker by the second.

Ever the professional, Dr. Wilkins responded graciously and smoothed over the difficult moment. Later, he would tell me that he secretly applauded my tenacity and drive. But it was a huge wake-up call for me. On our way back out to the car, my dad quietly said, "I don't care what you have been through, Kacey, you *never* have the right to treat people the way you just did. It is unacceptable." My heart sank. This straight-laced Daddy's girl had never been spoken to that way, but I deserved every ounce of the reprimand. Nothing about this new life resembled the old normal. I made it a priority to be much more aware of the way I spoke to others going forward.

The loss of my independence didn't go as quietly as I hoped it might. I had always been so self-sufficient; maybe this was a lesson in humility that I needed. Perhaps being forced into a situation where I was dependent on others would encourage emotional growth. At seventeen, though, I was having a hard time swallowing all of the humble pie, and I went through many boxes of tissues for my tears. I wanted to be that spunky, normal teenager who got to come and go as she pleased. Everyone seemed to be back to normal outside of the four walls of my home, and I felt the furthest thing from ordinary. I never felt angry per se, but the grief felt familiar to me. I had been through this rebuilding process a year earlier. Yet this seemed even harder.

In the summer of 1999, even though plans had been made to reopen Columbine High School to students in the fall, I began touring other high schools. My PTSD stood in the way of my return there. I needed a school building that felt comfortable to me so I could finish my senior year. I assembled a list of requirements: a small student body, a staff willing to warn me before fire drills so I could leave the building, and a facility in which each classroom had no less than two exits. My parents patiently took me from school to school, sometimes not understanding why a certain building felt unsafe to me. But they agreed that if a senior year was going to happen for me, it had to be in a place that I approved for reasons that only mattered to me. Finally, I settled on Denver Christian High School. I wasn't really happy about returning to ANY school, and I did not have that excitement most teenagers have about their senior year. The fastest way for me to escape the trauma that was high school was to suck it up and just finish. I wanted it over before it even began.

Of course, other frustrations bubbled up at the barn as a result of having to be an observer rather than a participant. Every weekend, I was attending horse shows to cheer on my sister and my peers. I sat on the sidelines, feeling skinny, weak, scarred, and broken.

They were able to continue competing and training; everything I was so passionate about was right at my fingertips, yet so far out of my reach. I wanted to be well, or at least able to fake that I was well. Maybe I could get away with riding. My surgeon would never know, right? But I knew deep down that it wasn't worth the risk. This was a one-of-a-kind shoulder Dr. Wilkins had painstakingly built for me, and I didn't dare destroy it. My donor was never far from my mind, either.

Perhaps even more painful than the shoulder wound itself was the torture they call physical therapy. Wow! I had hoped that the initial healing would cure the pain, but I was sorely mistaken. I spent what felt like too many hours in the PT's office, although I knew I desperately needed the therapy. My therapist, Marnie, was married to a trainer who had boarded my horse at one time; she was one of the kindest souls on the face of the earth. No one would ever know it, though, from the way she "treated" my injuries. Yes, it was her job, and yes, she did it to help me gain as much use of my arm and hand as possible. But OUCH.

The goal over the first six to eight weeks was to get the scar tissue to form around my wounds, allowing them to heal properly and in the right places. It seemed a bit counterintuitive for the next goal to be stretching out and breaking up that scar tissue in order to gain range of motion and function. I sat in Marnie's office, biting my tongue and cringing in agony as she massaged all my scars and then stretched first my thumb and then my arm in ways they did not want to move. Getting my thumb to move at all, much less to reach my index finger, was impossible at the beginning. But after months of therapy (read: torture), I was finally able to reach my pinky finger with my thumb. Then, it became a matter of building grip strength in the hopes of holding a pencil and writing again. As for my shoulder, it literally hung at my side at the start of therapy. After a year of work with Marnie,

I was able to lift it up to almost shoulder height, a range of motion that would slowly deteriorate over time. I was happy to move it at all, but honestly, quite devastated that I would never reach over my head again. I would not be able to put my hair into a ponytail without propping my right elbow up on a counter first to elevate my arm high enough to reach my hair.

While my friends were enjoying a senior year with their friends of four years, I was spending my time in physical therapy hoping to use my arm again, sleeping on my parents' bedroom floor, yearning to return to my equestrian pursuits, and learning more about my permanent disabilities. Even though I had a huge support group around me, I often felt lonely. Nobody understood the ongoing flashbacks, nightmares, fears, and irritations that I was experiencing. It wasn't that they didn't WANT to understand, but how could they? None of them had lived through what I had experienced. Nobody had witnessed things most people can only slightly imagine, and even then, just in black and white. I had full-color images and disturbing sound bites continually racing through my mind, beginning and repeating again and again and again. At seventeen, I wondered if it would always be that way.

I usually thought of victory as it related to a sporting event; the term normally refers to the healthy and fun conquering of an opponent. But the meaning of this word got twisted into something really ugly in the demented minds of the Columbine shooters.

Families of victims at Columbine were given the chance to view the "basement tapes," home movies that the two gunmen recorded before the shootings. In what I can only describe as tirades of hate, evil, and arrogance, I quickly learned what victory meant to those two boys: utter destruction. They did not care about surviving on April 20, Hitler's birthday. They were not hoping for relationship or growth with their classmates. Instead, they bragged how they intended to haunt our dreams forever. They hoped to kill as many people as possible. They laughed. They smirked. Showing mercy was definitely not part of their plan. They even took the time to dismiss their parents from all the blame. And, as I watched the videos, I realized something: they were winning in my life.

My dreams WERE haunted by them. Important parts of my body were destroyed. My "normal" life had been stolen from me, and my basic trust in the good of humanity was ripped out from underneath me. Instead of assuming the best, I found that I always assumed the worst. I was dependent on heavy drugs to sleep at night. The shooters had been largely successful in their twisted mission for dominion over my life. They may not have succeeded in killing me, but the damage they had done had the potential to alter the course of my life in irreversible ways.

Very quickly, I decided that I had a big decision in front of me. Would evil win? It didn't take me long to decide that, in MY life, the good was going to claim the victory. Those boys didn't deserve any more time in my dreams nor any continued power over my life. The hand on my back in the library was enough proof for me that God had power; that all the days ordained for me were written on His heart, and those days were meant for GOOD. I determined with God's strength inside of me that good would overcome evil.

It was my chance to start over. In the previous two years I had lost more friends than I could count on both hands. I decided I was finished with the sadness and heaviness in my life. Even though my heart was ready to move forward, my mind was still very broken. However, hope began to take root, and it began to take up a growing percentage of my thoughts. Regaining control of my life shot to the top of my priority list. Little did I know just how long that would actually take, but I would get there. There was no turning back.

In August of 1999, I was given clearance to participate in my first horse show with my restructured body. I was downright giddy with anticipation. I wasn't allowed to ride yet, but even competing in an event where I walked by my horse's side felt like freedom. I had spent the summer at the horse shows, bandaged up and fragile, and today was a day for participation, NOT observation!

That morning I had the chance to show in Showmanship, the class where I led the horse through a pattern of skills preselected by the judge. Getting dressed with my mom and my sister's help into my tight pants, sparkly shirt, belt buckle, dusty boots, and wide-brimmed white hat felt wildly liberating. I needed help with my makeup, and my sister helped me shape my hair into a tight bun. I knew this was one of my best and favorite events, but I was also keenly aware that I had to hold my hands and reins up for the whole course and the judge's subsequent inspection of my horse. I did not know when I began if I could hold the position for so long. Ironically, my recurring flaw in shows pre-Columbine was I tended to drop my right shoulder during events, a flaw that was now impossible! I was nervous and excited; full of hope that I would be as good as I was before the injury. I didn't want to let myself or anyone else down.

Word traveled fast. I noticed everyone got quiet as I stepped into the ring with my horse, and I knew the crowd was genuinely excited for my return to the competition circuit; the energy propelled me. Step by step, I showed my horse. And . . . I WON! I had not lost my mojo, and the shooters had not been able to steal my passion and determination. This began a watershed of small victories that fueled my recovery process, giving me new energy and emboldening my hope for the future. Fellow competitors and trainers knew the details of my difficult journey. My equestrian peers shared in the joy of my return to the show ring. Sometimes, it takes the cheerleading of an entire village to bring us back. Oh, how I needed my people.

In late August, I found myself buckled into my mom's car on the way to my first day at Denver Christian, filled with equal parts fear and excitement about starting a new chapter in my life. As expected, my day began with a heavy load of anxiety and fear resting squarely on my altered shoulders. Why on earth did I have to go back to school at all? Slinging my backpack over my left shoulder, realizing it was my only option, made me stop short in my tracks; I timidly walked the rest of the way to the front entrance. The door opened, and the principal greeted me warmly, but I immediately felt like the "Columbine Girl" whether I liked it or not. I knew it would be hard to overcome that identity and just be a regular student; I craved being regular so badly.

Walking down the senior hallway trying to find my locker, secretly looking for exits in every corridor, I felt the stares from my peers like hot lasers on my back. No one really knew how to behave around me, but to my classmates' credit, they gave it their best try that first day; I genuinely felt welcomed. I can't really blame them for not knowing exactly what to say or how to act. What teenager knows what to say in those circumstances? The gift of compassionate presence is the best present I have ever received, and I received plenty of it that day. I triumphantly skipped down my new school's steps that afternoon and grinned at my mom who was anxiously waiting in the car to drive me home. I had done it; I had really done it! I had successfully completed a day of school without a panic attack! Victory indeed.

Senior year continued uneventfully, thank goodness. Denver Christian opened their doors to my family in the midst of our grief, and they did so with grace and patience. My peers also rallied to provide a safe place where my broken mind would begin to heal, even offering to name me Homecoming Queen because of all I had been through. I respectfully declined their offer, not wanting to take the honor from a girl who truly deserved it, but I was so touched by the gesture. The teachers always warned me about upcoming fire drills, and new friends understood when I had to leave a room because of unexplainable anxiety. I was in an environment where I could begin to grasp that school might be a safe place again, and my parents took great comfort in that.

After I became comfortable at the school, I decided to play a little prank on some of the football players. Those big boys did not hold back their complaints on Monday mornings about the battle wounds they sustained in Friday night football games: dislocated shoulders, deep bruises, etc. I usually rolled my eyes at them, but not this time. I remembered that after my surgeries, my dad had tried to convince me the music I had imagined was actually playing through a signal from the metal in my shoulder. I decided to try that one on the football players. That sunny morning, I strolled into the senior hallway at Denver Christian, singing my heart out. I really should not be allowed to sing in public. When the football players asked what I was doing, I simply said, "I'm singing along with the music!"

Perplexed, they looked at each other and asked, "What music, Kacey?"

Straight-faced, I explained that I was able to receive radio signals through the metal grid in my shoulder. "Don't you hear it?" I said, bobbing my head along to the silent beat.

Of course, no one could hear it, hard as they tried. But for the rest of the day, I giggled hysterically to myself. I knew everybody was whispering to each other about whether or not this new girl could actually hear music through her shoulder like it was some kind of radio tower. Being the honest girl that I am, though, I could not continue the ruse for very long. But finding an opportunity to laugh at my new body was another sweet victory!

In fact, laughter was often the best medicine I took. The scars on the top of my shoulder left me with some numbness and nerve damage. I could never tell when I was being touched in that area. Brett was privy to this information, and he thought it was the funniest thing to stand behind me, tapping me on the shoulder while I sat there, oblivious. He cracked himself up while pestering me until he would yell, "BOO!" The belly laughs that ensued slowly helped with the healing. Brett often says that laughing kept him from crying; it still does.

As was to be expected, my parents remained in over-protective mode from the minute they found out I had been shot. Who could blame them? But these efforts sometimes impacted Britney and Brett. I know they look back sometimes with less than happy memories about the year before I was injured and the years after the tragedy.

Much was required from them that had nothing to do with their own personal growth. There is still some anger about what happened at Columbine floating around my family, specifically from my siblings. It comes out sideways sometimes, and I understand that. We all have our own process, and I honor that in their lives.

One day, Brett and I walked to a 7-Eleven down the street from our new school to grab Slurpees. While we were waiting to pay, two young men in black trench coats walked into the store, and the sight of their trench coats caused me to spill my Slurpee all over the floor. I yanked my brother out the door without paying for our drinks, my chest heaving. I'm pretty sure my brother felt as scared as I did.

No one in our family was untouched, and moving forward required every family member's participation. Britney was my caretaker much of that first year in the midst of her own equestrian training and school work. She is a naturally nurturing person, and I'm thankful for all the tender care she gave me physically and emotionally. I'm not sure I could have gone back to school or returned to competition without her daily support.

October of 1999 rolled in lazily, just like the leaves beginning to blow around my parents' property. The six months following the shooting had passed slowly and were mostly a blur of medical appointments. But I had been given enough training time at the barn to have clearance to compete in one of the most important competitions of the year: the Congress in Ohio. Brian traveled from Kentucky to join me for the weekend, and it is one of my favorite memories with him. Ever vigilant, we both refused to sit with our backs to the door in restaurants, sitting side by side in back booths making sure a path to an exit was clear.

That was the moment of truth: would my new body inhibit me from being a top-tier contender? Or, were my chances to get to the World Show in the summer of 2000 still a possibility? In the end, the weekend was a HUGE success. I never had more fun at a show. I savored the familiar smells of the barns and the palpable energy of the large-scale competition. I did not win, officially. But, in my heart of hearts, I did. My horse and I had a few amazing performances together; I felt strong and balanced. I knew that, given more time to train and regain my strength, I could still compete and win. Not only had I completed a whole weekend of competition, I had traveled without the security of my parents. At one point, it was something we thought might never happen again. Another victory.

My focused drive to compete in the World Show in the summer of 2000 grew intensely after that weekend in Ohio. I realized that in order to compete at the level I desired I needed a new horse. Moxie had gotten me through so much, but now I wanted to win at the highest level. Of course, I was careful to make sure Moxie went to a good home. The next few months were spent finding a new horse, Ryker. We drove to Texas with our trainer to find him; he was a gigantic, seventeen-hand, athletic, stunningly beautiful horse. It didn't matter to me that he was so tall; that is what made him so eye-catching. Of course, when I told Dr. Wilkins about Ryker, he just laughed. "Of course you went out and bought the biggest horse you could find, less than a year after I built you a brand new, customized shoulder!" He supported me, nonetheless. He said again, "Why fix your arm if I don't intend to let you use it?" I adore that man; he is one of my heroes.

The spring of 2000 ushered in new growth all around me. As the one-year anniversary of the shooting approached, my anxiety began to grow. Would I be more afraid on that day? Would the media hound me for interviews? I had quickly grown tired of the undesired attention coming my way. For nearly a year, complete strangers would notice and ask me about my unusual looking shoulder, bandages, and scars. I heard it all . . .

"How did you hurt your arm?"

"Oh my gosh, did your horse bite you?"

"Were you shot . . . with a GUN?!"

Usually my response was, "I was shot in the library at Columbine." Sometimes I avoided the truth to protect my privacy and just let people assume it was a car accident (the most common guess). But, when complete strangers heard my honest answer, I got to witness incredible kindness. It was true that Columbine really did touch our entire nation, not just everyone living in Littleton, Colorado, at the time. The shock on the faces of strangers was heartbreaking as they heard me recount how a quiet, young girl survived the worst school shooting in history up to that date. It was like I could see my own grief in their eyes. Many people just broke down crying. They often said, "I'm so sorry!" while giving me a warm hug as words failed them. But some people seemed to take a step back and really look at me. When they realized that I was genuinely okay, in a moment, their emotions changed right in front of me. "Oh, my goodness! Look at you! You look so great!" Victory indeed.

Even though I had climbed to the top of the leader board in my equestrian competitions, the excitement was dimmed a little by the looming one-year anniversary. I did not want to give my time to the media. I did not even know how to tell them what I felt quite yet. Was I happy to have survived? Guilty to have survived? Perhaps. Scared to experience the emotions again? Totally afraid of reliving the experience by recounting all the gory details? Most definitely.

Thankfully, for the one-year anniversary of the shooting, our family was offered a weekend away at the beautiful, historic Broadmoor Hotel in Colorado Springs. For a few days we were able to be together, tucked away from the busyness of the media storm and curious tourists in Littleton. We were given the freedom to spend the day however we needed to spend it as a family. We enjoyed togetherness, laughter, massages, and privacy. A much-needed gift.

One year had passed since the worst day of our lives, and we had sort of limped across the first finish line. We were tired. We were weary. But, at the same time, we were stronger and closer. And, I fully believed that I was going to make it in this world, perhaps the greatest victory of all. I wasn't anywhere close to the level of healing I desired, but I was fighting pretty hard to get there. And, I had a faith that was genuinely unwavering; my feet firmly planted. God was going to use all of my suffering to bless people and to honor the lives lost; I was convinced of that. And maybe, just maybe, He was even going to bless me in the chapters of my story that were yet to be written. As I walked across my high school graduation stage that May, thankful for a conclusion to a difficult year, I knew I would make sure none of my suffering got wasted. The pen was in my hand, and I was finally ready and willing to allow God to script the rest of my story.

Lacey Kacey

AQHA Horse Show, April 18, 1999

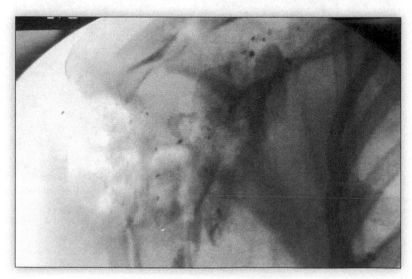

Shoulder X-ray 4/20/1999

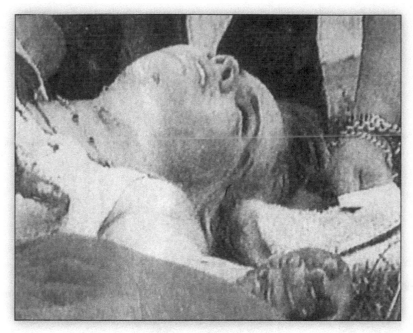

Triage, April 20, 1999

NSYNC visits Kacey in the hospital

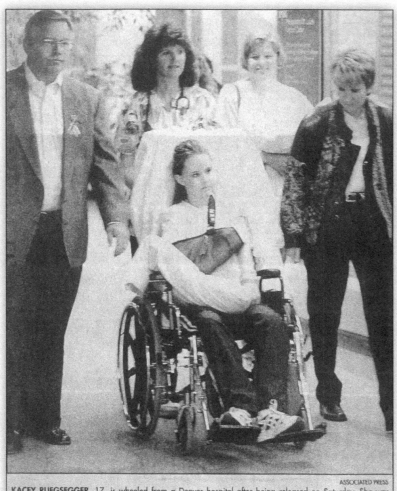

ASSOCIATED PRESS

KACEY RUEGSEGGER, 17, is wheeled from a Denver hospital after being released on Saturday. She was among the students wounded in the massacre at Columbine High School in Littleton. With her are her parents Greg, left, and Darcy, right. Hospital worker Patty Anderson is pushing the wheelchair.

Kacey is released from the hospital

Mural painted for Kacey by a homeless man

Rose Parade Engagement

Patrick and Kacey

Greg and Darcey Ruegsegger, on Kacey's wedding day

Dr. Ross Wilkins and Kacey

Kacey introducing her daughters to their brother

Kacey speaking in Denver

Patrick, Kacey, Mallory, Logan, Bentley, and Corban

The Johnson kids walking through life together

CHAPTER 7

TATTOOS OF SURVIVAL

August 2000. Fort Worth, Texas. American Quarter Horse World Show. Hand-sewn, blindingly bright sequins glittering on the most exquisite show costumes. The shiniest, most exquisitely designed saddles on the market. Pristine new hats atop every head. The strongest and most competent quarter horses in the world. The "yes, ma'ams" and "y'alls" dripping out of nearly every mouth. The wafting familiar smells of stables and Texas street food. I walked around wide-eyed as we arrived in the blistering summer heat, like a little girl in a giant candy store trying to take in the wonder of it all. I let every ounce of the blood, sweat, and tears of my accomplishment wash over me as I headed to the registration tables. Banged up me—a registered participant in what to me was the greatest horse show on earth! In my wildest imagination, I never could have dreamed up anything so spectacular.

Hot months spent at the barn, as well as traveling to multiple competitions that summer, helped me to feel somewhat normal again. I got to do what I loved, and I had a fair amount of success at it. It took a lot more effort for me than my peers to compete in something so physically demanding, but it assisted in rebuilding my strength, mentally and physically. And, as per usual, I was a workaholic. While my bubbly younger sister continued to build strong friendships at the barn, I was laser focused on my goals and somewhat isolated from my peers. The World Show preparation trumped nearly everything in my life.

Ryker and I had busted our tails off to get an invitation to this party of all equestrian parties; I was dressed in my best clothes, boots, and hat, hungry to just get out there and compete! To think that just sixteen months before, I had nearly bled to death on the floor of the Columbine library. My accomplishments felt electric; the energy was literally pouring out of me. What had been intended to ruin my life had instead fueled it, culminating in my inclusion at this pinnacle event.

I walked up to the tables and gathered my paperwork, anxious to check on Ryker and his accommodations. I had qualified to represent Colorado in four events at the World Show. As they had done for so many of Brett's hockey tournaments, my family flew to Texas to be my cheering section. The opening ceremonies at the World Show are similar to the Olympic Opening Ceremonies, chock-full of pageantry. Each state parades its smartly dressed participants around the ring as they show off matching outfits to the huge crowd. I savored every second of it, a lump the size of an apple in my throat. Nothing about the experience was lost on me.

A month before the show, Ryker got hurt. He was near the end of his competition career and fell lame on one of his front legs. My trainers worked tirelessly to heal him, as they knew how much I needed this experience to help in my healing. Working outside of his job description, my trainer, Tom, dedicated extra hours every day to nursing Ryker back to health. One afternoon, I went to the barn to practice on a different horse while Ryker was receiving treatments. Tom wanted me to gain an appreciation for how much my horse had to endure in therapy to make my dream come true. So, as Ryker stood in the aisle of the barn with his front hoof submerged in a bucket of ice water, Tom sat me on a bucket next to him to do the same. I gingerly put my foot in the bucket. It hurt like crazy, until the numbness kicked in.

I quickly realized exactly what Tom was trying to teach me. I wasn't the only one who had worked to make it this far. Success was a team effort, and I unfortunately had lost sight of that a little bit. My trainers and my horse had made so many sacrifices to help me achieve my goal. The ice bucket was a bonding experience for

Ryker and me; I needed the humbling eye-opener. Just as I had given everything I had despite a severe injury, so my horse would also rise to the occasion through adversity. We were a team.

Ryker was still not in fighting form when we moved toward the entrance of the ring for the first time at the World Show. My heart was pounding out of my chest, and I tried to keep the sweat off my brow as my emotions threatened to tip my concentration. To be the best at a show, the rider must "know" they are the best. Entering the show pen for our Hunter Under Saddle event, I could feel the judges' critical eyes on me. I sensed in my spirit that the massive animal underneath me was not completely right, so after whispering a quick prayer, I nudged Ryker along and poised myself in the saddle to give the impression we had what it took to win. I had competed enough to know, though, that we wouldn't advance to the next round based on the competition I had carefully observed. What we gave instead was OUR very best. Maybe on another day we would have gotten better results, but there was no reason to be disappointed. As we exited the arena, I leaned forward and softly laid my head on Ryker's neck, hugging him as tears streaked down my cheeks. I lovingly whispered in his ear that he did so very well, that WE did so very well. There is absolutely no shame in giving your best and not coming out on top.

And we did give our best, three more times. We made it through four performances together in Fort Worth. We didn't win any of the top prizes, but that didn't matter to me. Neither one of us was physically at the top of our game. We gave everything we had as a team, though, and I left the competition draped in gratitude.

It was clear after the World Show that Ryker needed to be put out to pasture. He had put in ten grueling years of intense competition, a true athlete in every sense of the word.

Ryker was ready for a show horse's royal retirement, free to roam the pastures and graze on fresh, green grass. Selling him reduced me to tears, but I knew it was time. Ryker's continued struggle to heal from his injuries helped me make the difficult decision. And, to my great surprise, I felt finished with my equestrian career, too. I recognized that I was ready to embrace a new season in my life. I was preparing to leave for college, and I knew I needed to be free from the intensity of my goals at the barn.

I realized I just wanted out. Like a heavy blanket that grows too warm to be truly comfortable, all the protection my family had offered me began to feel like heat stroke. I wanted to be normal. Everyone knew it was a stretch for me to attend a college even ninety minutes away from my parents' home, so I never even considered leaving the state for my education. Colorado State University (CSU) is located north of Denver, nestled in the cute town of Fort Collins. It was also closer to Greeley where Ryker was kept, his sale not yet finalized; he felt like family to me. CSU was a large university, and I thought its size would provide me with the anonymity I craved. I wanted to leave the "Columbine Girl" and all of her troubles at home.

I had never been away from home, except to compete at horse shows, and that usually included the safety net of my family. The advertised student life at CSU seemed exactly what I was looking for; it would allow me the freedom I thought I needed for the next chapter of my life. I was excited to be unwound from the (understandably) controlling tethers of my parents, but mostly, just anxious to lose the chains of the tumultuous life from the previous three years. Funny how what you think you want and what you actually need are sometimes two different things. But nobody could have told me that at the time.

I signed up for a full schedule of credits, unsure of what kind of degree I wanted to earn. After the initial shock of living with strangers in a new environment began to wear off, I mostly enjoyed going to class. The campus felt very different from the atmosphere in the high schools I attended. The size of the lecture halls made me feel more comfortable and less trapped. I could spot the exit doors with ease. The classes were interesting, too; I achieved good grades without having to try very hard. I felt sort of aimless, though, which was in stark contrast to the life I had known before.

It was the nightlife that became my greatest teacher. Except for my sophomore year at Bear Creek High School, I did not have much exposure to drinking or parties. I thought, "Why not see what this is all about?" So, I quickly found myself attending parties around campus, enjoying the typical college atmosphere. I drank, and sometimes I drank a lot. I walked and sometimes stumbled around the streets of Fort Collins with my friends in the early morning hours, feeling free from Columbine and all my labels. I let myself get lost with other college kids. Alcohol was such a wonderful numbing agent, but it came with a steep price.

Eventually, my brain went numb. I was irresponsible. Truly, though, it wasn't even that fun for me; I just didn't know what else to do. The partying helped to anesthetize my emotional and mental pain, but deep down, I knew my behavior would not lead to the trajectory I wanted for my life. The decisions I made on a regular basis embarrassed me, and certainly would have embarrassed my family if I had been completely transparent. I hung out a lot with my childhood friend, Derek, and his roommate; the familiarity made me feel somewhat comfortable and safe. But mostly, I felt like a foreigner in these new college clothes. Nothing fit quite right.

Late one night, I was drinking in a dorm room with my friends and playing cards. Out of nowhere, the cops showed up. When an officer asked me to say and then spell my name, I could not do it. In my defense, most people can't spell Ruegsegger when they are sober! I felt humiliated. I wanted to tell the officer, "This isn't me! I don't do this! You have the wrong impression of me!" I went back to my room with a ticketed warning in hand, hot with shame. From that night forward, I left the party lifestyle behind me.

In preparation for second semester, I arranged my schedule to allow for long weekends at home in Littleton. I was in Fort Collins Tuesday through Thursday, which gave me the freedom to be at my parents' house Friday through Monday. This felt much more comfortable to me. I was thankful to have experienced a taste of the wild life just so I was firmly convinced it wasn't what I wanted. It took a three-month experiment for me to understand that there was more to my impending adulthood than partying with my peers. The years I had been given back in the library at Columbine were not going to be wasted partying; I would make sure of that. I began to understand my responsibility to steward the gift of life I had graciously been given by God. Some of my peers in the library never got that option; I resolved to make the most of it.

As I spent more time at home on the weekends, I was able to focus on my new direction. What should I do with myself? How was I going to rewrite my script? I went through a few months of thinking I would go to beauty school after I figured out that a degree in early childhood education was not for me. Why I thought working in a school would be a good idea for someone with my "issues" is beyond me! The beauty school idea was squashed when I realized I could not hold my arm up long enough to cut or color someone's hair. The thought kept coming back to me: I want to make a difference with the story of my life. So, I focused on the people who had made a strong impression on me. As I processed my experiences, I always went back to the nurses who cared for me during my hospital stays. They worked day and night to help our family through the hardest days of our lives, leaving permanent stamps of compassion and empathy on our hearts.

That was it. I would train to be a nurse. Even better, I would be a Pediatric Oncology nurse! Young cancer patients have inspiring amounts of courage, and I knew a thing or two about courage. So, after completing my freshman year, I withdrew from CSU and moved back home to my parents' house. I finished my required prerequisites at Arapahoe Community College (ACC).

ACC was only fifteen minutes from my house, and I appreciated the privacy in my parents' large finished basement more than ever. When I finished my prerequisites, I had to make a decision about pursuing an associate's degree (RN) or a Bachelor of Science in Nursing (BSN). From what I had been told, the bachelor's degree would provide more opportunity for working in leadership, including but not limited to jobs as a nursing supervisor or nurse educator. None of that mattered to me. I wanted to be at the bedside, completely hands-on with the people who needed my attention. I had no interest in being anyone's boss or supervisor. The thought of providing hope, comfort, patience, and understanding to others brought my heart a lot of joy.

Choosing a career gave me a new motivation to move forward. My year at CSU had been rather aimless, mostly an escape of sorts. It helped my healing process to purposely spend my days poring over books and working out complicated lab findings in the safety and comfort of my own home. School almost became normal for me, although I never stepped foot into the ACC library. I would ask friends or classmates to get what I needed if there was ever a need for library resources. Very soon after the shooting, I told myself I would never set foot in a library again.

My daily routine was mundane, but it made me feel perfectly safe. I attended classes, worked at retail jobs or at my dad's law office, studied in my parents' basement while watching hockey games, and even attended a college youth group. The college church group was more about having fun than probing spiritual depths, if I'm honest. But it provided me with a community and a social outlet. The healthy new friendships built my trust in people again. Most of us had taken turns dating each other, too; we were an energetic group of young adults who did everything together. Finally, a positive and healthy environment!

The group met at the church on Tuesday nights. And, just like high school, my parents' house became the gathering place for us to hang out after church. With a large walkout basement that included a pool table, kitchen area, poker and foosball tables, and a large-screen TV, the basement was the perfect place for all of us to eat, play games, and laugh together. Most of the group knew our house as their second home. Weekends were spent going to movies, hanging out at parks, and any other random outdoorsy activities we could dream up. I was thankful for the social network.

Our group traveled to California, New York, New Jersey, and even took a Caribbean cruise together. The joyful time we spent as a unit made us a pretty tight-knit crew. Thank goodness for those intimate friendships because in a moment nobody could have scripted, we had to hold onto each other for dear life and pray.

After landing in Miami, Florida, as the sun was setting over the beautiful blue water on a warm night in May 2003, our group embarked on our second cruise together. We were headed for seven days in the sunny, laid-back eastern Caribbean. I was so excited; a carefree week full of fancy dinners, games, dance parties, lazy pool days, and cliff jumping. It was going to be a college student's dream vacation. We laughed and joked our way through the safety drills shortly after boarding the ship; I felt more invincible than I had in a long time. I nearly skipped to my cabin to unpack my swimsuits, shorts, and tank tops. This was my idea of paradise!

The trip lived up to my expectations. We enjoyed dressing up in old prom gowns for five-course dinners, giggling as we tried to figure out which fork to use for each course. We played pranks on each other and embraced all the adventure the ship's crew had to offer us. My skin was glowing and I'm not sure I ever felt happier in my life.

The last night of the cruise inched up on us; we dreaded packing our damp swimsuits and dirty tank tops. Tomorrow would bring a long day of travel home to Colorado. So we laid out on the deck of the ship late that night and savored every last minute of the vacation. We grudgingly found our beds late that evening; I never wanted to leave.

BOOM. The ship shakes us right out of our early morning sleep, and my feet hit the ground. The explosion is so loud, I am certain a bomb has gone off just outside our door. It is happening again—this one in a million situation has found me all the way out here on the water! What on earth is happening!? Are there people on board with bombs? Guns? Did our ship crash into a rock? Alarms are sounding, and my blood pressure is steadily rising to match the panic onboard the ship. Groggy and clad in pajamas, everyone in our group is ordered to our lifeboat stations, and then instructed to secure our life vests. The drill that nobody ever takes seriously is now vitally important to our survival—why did I mess around during the presentation? Here I am AGAIN, trapped in a situation from which I cannot escape. My heart is pounding.

My mind runs wild. How can something like this possibly be happening? I quickly find my friend who had also been in the Columbine library; his sister held the shirt to my bleeding shoulder as we waited outside of the school right after the shooting. He immediately knows I need comfort. As we huddle with our group, waiting for the impending evacuation orders, my friend holds his arms around my trembling body. He lovingly provides the understanding that only a fellow survivor of Columbine can offer me. I know we are either going to sink or be blown to bits. I'm sure I am going to be fish food within minutes.

For me, a massive panic attack can be triggered by anything. There are the obvious triggers—men wearing trench coats, fireworks, the smell of gunpowder, big backpacks, sirens, cars backfiring, doors slamming, and suspicious-looking people. But it is this last trigger— suspicious-looking people—that others who have not been victimized don't always understand. Things that stand out as suspicious to me appear completely normal to most people. Oftentimes, I cannot explain what or who triggers a reaction. An attack involves a sure feeling of doom: trembling hands, hypervigilant vision, racing heart, fight or flight response, and an inability to process words or situations with any amount of reason. More often than not, these attacks do not subside unless I am far removed from the situation. And, usually, an attack means the rest of the day is ruined; completely drained of all my energy and my sense of safety, I cannot remain in public.

I'm having one right now. I am exposed, and I have nowhere to go.

Although I am sure it has been mere minutes, it feels like hours until we are led off the ship. I survive the panic attack; I am guided off the large vessel in a daze. We do not have any of our luggage, and nothing looks familiar. There is no time for the evacuation to function normally. We learn that a massive blast of high-pressure steam in the boiler room on the aft end of the ship has tragically taken the lives of four people. Although no passengers have been hurt, twenty-one crew members have been seriously injured, some jumping to safety in the deep water below the ship, and thirteen of them are listed in critical condition. Just unbelievable. I can't process any of it. I will never get on a ship again; this I know for sure.

Our vacation is quickly blanketed by a very heavy feeling of sadness, something I recognize. The people who lost their lives had just finished working to provide us with a weeklong vacation of fun in the sun. And now, in an instant, their lives on this earth are finished. All I can think about are the families who will be left behind, the bereaved who now must deal with the unimaginable. Well, unimaginable to some, but not to me.

As we wait in silence for a ride to the airport, I quickly think of my mom. I feel like I am in the ambulance again. If she has seen this story on the news, she knows for sure that I am on that exact ship. She will panic, and rightly so. I hurry to find someone with a cell phone, so I can call to reassure her before she is blindsided with another report of her daughter being in the middle of an unbelievable tragedy. As soon as she answers, I calmly say, "Mom, don't panic. Our ship had a huge explosion. We are okay. I'm okay. We are no longer on the ship, and we will still be flying home today, I think. I can't wait to see you. I need to see you." I can hear her breathing heavily into the phone. How many phone calls like this can one mother take? She just cannot make sense of any of it. As expected, the relief is overwhelming; I can hear her quietly crying into the receiver. I don't even remember getting on the plane and could not collapse into my parents' arms fast enough at Denver International Airport. I was home.

The explosion on the ship was yet another reminder of how precious life truly is; how in an instant, things can change, and people can be taken from you. With my feet firmly planted on Colorado soil, I focused my thoughts on my future. I was excited to complete my nursing degree. I knew my gifts of compassion and empathy could be used for good, that all my suffering would not be in vain. It was a real starting point for me.

The limitations of my shoulder had not greatly hindered my ability to care for patients during my nursing clinicals. Except for the occasional assistance I needed to raise heavy IV bags high up onto the pole, I was proficient in my tasks. I never felt embarrassed by my damaged body; working with others whose bodies weren't functioning properly, I was actually proud of my physical scars. They felt like permanent tattoos of survival that brought me closer to my patients. The shadowy ridges of the scars on my heart and mind were harder to see and certainly proved more difficult to heal, but they didn't hold me back from doing good work.

Slowly, I began to believe that I might be able to calm the fears that lurked at the surface of my thoughts nearly every day. Maybe I would eventually think like a normal person again. Hiding out and avoiding circumstances that made me feel uncomfortable were not propelling me forward; that was very obvious. Certainly, I could not reroute my thoughts by myself, though. So, I continued to lean on my support group, as well as that ever-present Hand that had shielded me in my moment of terror in the library. I trusted that God in His sovereignty had good things in store for my life, albeit by a circuitous, painful route. I knew deep in my bones that something good was going to come out of my experiences. That knowledge helped me through some of my darkest days; I genuinely believed I would get out from underneath the paralyzing negativity. I wanted my suffering to count for something good.

I purposely chose to stay out of the dating scene for about ten months. It provided me the time and space I needed to get reacquainted with myself, to figure out what kind of person I wanted to be and what sort of person I wanted to marry. My folks have a great marriage; a life-long marriage has always been one of my life goals. I like being in a relationship more than being alone.

My dad has always been one of my heroes, and I knew I wanted to marry someone like him. I wanted a man who loved God with his whole heart first and foremost; a man who was fully dedicated to loving his wife and family as a second priority. My mom began to tease me, asking when I was finally going to settle down and marry someone. I dated a lot in my younger years, and she was always wondering which guy I was going to pick!

On a hot day in early June 2003, I told my mom, "You know, I don't think I have met the person I will marry yet. I don't think it is one of the guys at church who is already a friend. I really think God will bring a new person to church, and I will just know."

She knew my type. Tall, slender build, blonde hair, light eyes. Funny, yet understated, never wanting to be the center of attention. Obviously, since Avalanche player Peter Forsberg had not called, God was going to have to work some magic and bring along somebody really special to get my attention.

Within a college group where everyone has dated everyone else, any time a new guy or girl steps through the door, people jump at the opportunity to make the first connection. As more of a quiet observer than a gregarious flirt, this was not a skill I possessed.

However, the old adage "when you know, you know" is true, I guess. A girl is going to go after what she wants; I was no exception. It was a regular Tuesday night, and he walked right through the doorway and into my life.

No, no, ladies. MOVE over, because this one is mine! The minute he sauntered into the church with his buddy, I made a not so subtle announcement to anyone listening that this guy was MINE. Who does that? Not me, not ever! I couldn't help it, though. I knew the other girls would be all over this new guy, and I had to act fast. He was incredibly good-looking, witty, and fun—exactly my type! Shy Kacey was not going to be shy tonight.

I played it just right. I pretended to be outgoing and walked right up to introduce myself. Then, I arranged for the larger group to gather at my parents' house later that night, hoping this Patrick Johnson might stop by. He did, and for me, the rest is history. He won't admit it, but he was already pretty hooked, too.

The rest of that summer, we worked on our tans at the swimming pool, barbecued at friends' houses, and played pool at my house with Patrick and his friends. The friendship grew slowly, but the attraction was always there. I had dated enough to know that this guy possessed qualities I was looking for in a husband. It was an added bonus that he didn't feel too intimidated by spending time with my dad. He invested a lot of time in my family, winning their hearts over slowly but surely.

Patrick was just a different breed of boyfriend, and I knew it pretty quickly. All of his thoughts and actions were well-intentioned and purposeful; he was wise and even-keeled. This was exactly the kind of man I wanted: a steady, calm presence. He immediately embraced my past, my physical deficits and the broken pieces in my mind that still needed fixing, trusting that a brighter future was ahead. In fact, I attribute much of my healing to his partnership. He taught me a lot about facing my fears in those early months of our relationship, and his new perspective on the dark events in my life was refreshing.

As nursing school got more intense, the workload and demand for resources increased. I needed to be in the library with my classmates researching and studying to complete my degree. It was clear that my "never" statement wasn't going to hold water for much longer. But I was often so frozen with fear that I would walk into the airy library space, only to see a table resembling the one I had hid under years before and find myself running back to my car in an absolute panic.

Patrick was so patient and willing to spend the time I needed to ease back into a library setting. He would walk in before me, look around and find a "safe" place for me to settle where I could clearly see the exits. Then, I would walk in and he would keep watch as I frantically completed my work. Every effort he extended made it a little easier the next time. We would go get ice cream or coffee to celebrate the little hurdle I had hopped over. These weren't little hurdles to me, though. They were giant strides in my healing. He applied the same energy to helping me in restaurants and stores when I felt afraid, giving me "normal person reality" and helping me assess my surroundings through his regular lenses instead of the skewed view I usually saw first. People were just trying to eat or shop; they were not trying to kill me.

Spending time with Patrick and his family gave me a new perspective. Up until that point, the majority of people in my life had been by my side through the suicides, the tragedy at Columbine, multiple surgeries, panic attacks, horse shows, and mental healing. This new family knew nothing of my pain and very little of my suffering. They were aware of my physical disabilities, but they were unable to fully grasp the extent of my mental and emotional brokenness because they had not been a part of the suffering my family had endured. While some of this was refreshing—I felt like I had a clean slate—I also craved for them to understand the scope of everything; even Patrick could not fully understand. His family had no way to comprehend the tremendous amount of healing I had experienced in the five years since the shooting. It created some tension between Patrick and me.

Six months into our relationship, Patrick and I needed a break. I was not a girlfriend with an easy story, and unique challenges were in play as I clawed my way back to emotional and mental health. We both needed to step back and gather some perspective about our future. It was the summer before my last semester of nursing school, and I wanted to have some fun. So I made a spur-of-the-moment decision to move to California to live with my Aunt Sherry for the summer. Patrick drove me out to Irvine where I planned to share a two-bedroom condo with my aunt. I was just ten minutes from the beaches in Laguna—total paradise. Patrick and I said our awkward goodbyes and I watched him drive away with tears in my eyes. I think I knew I would see him again, but we needed some time apart to focus on ourselves as individuals. All by myself for perhaps the first time in my life, and with all the time in the world to think, I was ready to embrace new growth.

I didn't take a job for the first time in many summers. I spent my time walking the shoreline, reading my Bible, listening to music, and missing Patrick. I knew this was potentially my last extended period of relaxation before my career would really begin, and I was tired. Really tired. Palm trees swayed in the ocean breezes, bright sunshine and sandy beaches greeted me each morning, and I loved every moment in my favorite environment. The distance was good for Patrick and me, but it wasn't like we really took a break from each other. We used the time to build a stronger foundation for our relationship. Physical space gave us time to really talk to each other on the phone, to listen well, and to laugh over the silliest things. We were both intentional about seeking God's plan for our relationship; we spent a lot of time in quiet prayer.

As our conversations grew more serious in nature, our distance proved more difficult. I never wanted to leave California, but my life was in Colorado, and despite the helpful break from familiar places and routines, I knew I needed to go home. I had no choice but to return to school—I could almost taste the thrill of the dean handing over my diploma. I began to think about my departure.

Patrick was always thoughtful and romantic during our separation, making sure to keep my attention. One night, we had a silly date planned. It was just a regular movie night that involved him calling me after work, chatting on the phone for a few minutes, and then separately watching a movie—him on his couch in Colorado, me on mine in California. But I was completely unaware of his plans to be sure I was at the condo that night.

He didn't call until almost 10:00 p.m. I was in my pajamas with a freshly scrubbed face, my hair piled high on my head in a messy bun, just laying around waiting for the phone call to interrupt the late-night silence. I picked up on the second ring, anxious to hear his warm voice. He casually asked, "Hey, where are you?"

I told him I was at the condo, and then punctuated it with a loud, "Duh!"

He said, "Well, I'm at the airport waiting for a ride to see you. I'm taking you back to Colorado, dang it. Come pick me up!"

"What?!" I screamed before slamming the phone back into its cradle. I threw on some shorts and a tank top, grabbing my flip-flops as I raced out to my car. I drove like a wild woman all the way to the airport, barely putting the car in park before jumping out of the driver's seat and flinging myself into his arms. We went straight to Laguna Beach to walk around and spent the early morning hours daydreaming about our plans for the last days of summer in Colorado. I truly felt at home with him, and my heart felt enduringly fixed with his. I just knew. After a fun-filled, relaxing week together, we made our way back to Colorado. We were so young and naive, and yet very much in love. Absence indeed made our hearts grow permanently fonder.

The fall of 2004 was just out-and-out fun. I finished up nursing school and realized it was exactly what I wanted to do with my life. I graduated in December, just before the holidays. Standing in the middle of the intersection where my abilities and talents met real-world work opportunities felt victorious. After several nerve-wracking interviews, I landed a job that would start in a few months at Littleton Adventist Hospital. I knew I would be able to provide my patients with the same calm and positivity that Patrick provided for me in my life outside of work. I was in love with my dream man, looking forward to spending hours doing purposeful work with inspiring patients; life finally seemed to be matching my expectations.

A few weeks after I graduated, I had the great privilege of riding on the Donate Life Float in the famous Rose Parade in Pasadena, California. Months earlier, AlloSource (the company that donated the bones used to save my arm and thumb) had requested to sponsor me as a tissue recipient on the flower-filled float. My sister and I had the chance to ride in the parade on the same float as other organ and tissue recipients and families of donors.

It was an honor that I had no intention of refusing. And a trip to sunny California during the Colorado winter? Yes, please! Most of my family flew to Pasadena to join us for the festivities. We enjoyed meticulously decorating the float with thousands of gorgeous pink and yellow flowers with our new friends. This event was just the beginning of my eyes being opened to the widespread impact that tissue donation has on the lives of recipients and donor families. Unbeknown to me, just when I thought being in the parade couldn't get any more exciting, there was something in the works behind the scenes that would impact my life in a significant way.

The morning of New Year's Eve, after a few stressful hours completing the design of the float with flowing white orchids, I was flat-out grouchy. I snapped at Patrick more than once. I was tired and overwhelmed with all the attention, and the speech I had to give at a donation event that night was weighing heavily on me. I was so nervous about standing in front of such a large crowd. To brighten my mood, Patrick had a huge bouquet of flowers delivered to my room while I was getting ready for the evening. The beautiful arrangement dramatically changed my attitude. He knew me so well; I felt seen and cherished. I slipped into my burgundy-and-black lace gown, took one last peek in the mirror at my side-swept up-do, and headed to the ballroom downstairs.

After enjoying appetizers and wine, all the Donate Life participants were given the chance to share their stories in front of hundreds of guests. I sat rapt with attention as each survivor shared the beauty of tissue donation in its many forms, and the ball of nerves inside of me loosened up a bit. Patrick kept getting up to use the bathroom, which I thought was kind of weird. Last in the line-up, my sister and I gave a short version of my story, and then returned to our seats. As soon as I sat down, the emcee called me back to the stage. I had no clue what was going on; my guess was that it was some kind of media opportunity. Promised a "special presentation" by the host, I slowly returned to the front of the room and walked up the stairs to the stage. Then, I turned to the left to see my Patrick standing beside me with a guitar. Wait, what?

This could NOT be happening. I had NO IDEA! It only took a second to figure out that he must be on stage to propose. When it registered in my head, the waterworks started. He serenaded me with *The Blower's Daughter* as he strummed the guitar. I will never forget the beautiful things he said about why he wanted to marry me. Then he dropped to one knee and asked me to be his wife. By this point, I was a blubbering mess. Tears of joy flowed down my cheeks and smeared my makeup. Obviously, I said, "YES!" to thunderous applause from my family and fellow guests. My new diamond ring sparkled back at me in the candlelit ballroom, reflecting all the love and light I felt in my heart.

It was a moment I will never forget for as long as I live. Even though a more private proposal at the lookout point near Laguna Beach, where we had spent hours eating ice cream and dreaming about our future together, would have been much more our style, Patrick seized my involvement in the once-in-a-lifetime Rose Parade to create an unforgettable memory. He spent months coordinating with the Donate Life event planners to make sure all the details were in order. They provided a guitar that was strategically resting on its stand on the stage that did not seem out of place, which kept Patrick from driving to California with a guitar in tow. That would have made me very suspicious. He also made sure I was the last recipient to share my story so the evening would conclude with his proposal. Word traveled fast. The hotel graciously provided chocolate-covered strawberries and chilled champagne that we enjoyed on their rooftop deck after the reception concluded. The fireworks in Pasadena that night mirrored the explosions of sheer love and joy I felt in my soul.

My dear man kept his plan for the proposal a secret for months, but not before braving a stressful lunch with my dad. Earlier in September, Patrick asked my dad to join him for lunch to talk business. Dad knew better; this was NOT about business, and he simply refused Patrick's invitation. He wasn't ready to let me go, not after what we had been through together. Patrick was persistent, though, and weeks later Dad begrudgingly agreed to a meeting. Dad knew what was coming before arriving to the deli that day, but he wasn't sure he was ready for his little princess to be whisked away by her Prince Charming. Not that he ever had a choice in the matter, but still.

As they sat at the table awkwardly chomping on their sandwiches, Patrick nervously began to tell Dad his intentions for our relationship, and eventually asked for my hand in marriage. We joke that it's a miracle Patrick became my husband, because my dad's emotions got in the way and he never actually said yes! His lack of response was not because he didn't approve of Patrick, but giving his daughter away was more than his heart could handle at the moment. I'm not exactly sure how the lunch ended, but I know the tension was thick. My dad had to call Patrick on his drive back to the office to finally give his permission and apologize for his hesitation.

Newly engaged and on cloud nine, I bounded out of bed early on the morning of the Rose Parade. The energy in the staging area was electric; I felt deeply honored to be included on a float that represented something so important to me. My sister and I spent most of our time riding on the float in our pink sweaters staring at the new ring on my finger; we couldn't stop fantasizing about my big wedding. I was the girl who had survived the unthinkable, but now I was in love and finally living my dream. I had a permanent grin on my face as we rode the float down the storied Colorado Boulevard. When we passed by the television crews, an announcer spilled the beans of our engagement for CBS viewers, including some of my family members watching across the country, and sealed our story for posterity.

It quickly became clear that we wanted a short engagement. The week after the parade, we lounged in California as a family and talked of nothing but the upcoming wedding. I think I literally floated the thousand miles back to Colorado.

We picked May 14 for our big day, not wanting to wait until the only remaining September date at my parents' country club. I searched long and hard for an old-fashioned church with stained glass and a long, central aisle; we settled on First Presbyterian Church of Littleton. Details began to fall into place slowly but surely that cold and snowy spring, and I enjoyed coordinating everything with my red, black, and white theme. My dream of a classy, candlelit event began to take shape.

I started my new job as an oncology nurse on the seventh floor at Littleton Adventist Hospital in March 2005. As a newly minted graduate, I knew I had a lot to learn, but putting on my fresh scrubs that first day felt like such a full-circle moment. I would be on the other side of the bed now, caring for very sick patients. It was my intention to wholeheartedly pour myself into the people I had the blessing of caring for each day. With two preceptors to lead me, I enjoyed the fast pace and high expectations of the hospital administration in striving for excellence in patient care. Gaining the respect of my fellow nurses and doctors as well as the hospital chaplain was very important to me. Going to work was an absolute joy in the midst of a pretty busy season of my life preparing to be a bride and new wife. It felt great to channel my life experience into something positive.

Finding real purpose for all the pain in my life felt powerful. Providing care for suffering patients grew what started as a flickering fire of interest into an all-out blaze. I completely related to people in pain, which made it easy for me to empathize and communicate an unspoken understanding with patients and their families. The sicker the patients, the stronger my connection to them. The work was hard, and the hours long, but the satisfaction incredibly deep.

My mom let me pick things for the wedding to my taste and didn't impose her opinions on me, for which I was very thankful. Her planning assistance was invaluable to us. Patrick and I handled our busy work schedules while looking for a new apartment to live in after we married. My dad was fully supportive, too, and wanted everything to be perfect. The four of us enjoyed cake tasting and choosing a dinner menu at Pinehurst Country Club together.

I wasn't quite sure what kind of wedding dress I wanted, but I knew when I put on "The One" that I would just know it. I went to three different stores in the Denver area with my sister and my mom to try on white bridal gowns. I never once considered my scarred shoulder, and that felt strangely triumphant. When I found the creamy, strapless princess gown with subtle lace accents and tiny buttons down the back, it just felt right. When I brought my dad to the store to show it to him, he cried when he saw me in it. I cried, too, as the sales lady placed the traditional arm-length veil on my head; I was really going to get married! It became real for me after my bridal shower hosted by a family friend, Hunter Olson. The excitement was building.

Two weeks before our big day, Patrick and I plopped on opposite ends of the couch in our young pastor's office. Despite only counseling and then marrying one other couple before us, our pastor did an incredible job coaching us through a major disagreement. We were stressed at the time and battling with each other over minor things. We were never one of those perfect couples who agreed on everything, and that was fine by me. Patrick and I realized sitting on that couch that we were dealing with a lot: new jobs, finding a new home, wedding planning, and the always-there issues surrounding my healing. We left that counseling session with more grace for each other, excited about our new life together. Perfection wasn't our goal; honest, sacrificial love motivated us.

Ever the sportsman, a week before the wedding, Patrick asked my opinion about his participation in a fast-pitch softball tournament with his dad. I quickly responded with a resounding, "No!" as I was afraid of a potential injury. He assured me he had never been hurt in a softball game in his life. I said again, "NO!"

We compromised. On the Monday night before the wedding, instead of accepting the invitation to play in the fast-pitch game, Patrick and his dad instead filled in on my dad's slow-pitch softball game with my blessing. I worked a thirteen-hour shift that day; exhausted, I walked to my car while fumbling for my phone in the bottom of my purse. I looked down and saw that I had missed seven calls from Patrick.

I called him immediately.

He said, "Kacey, meet us at urgent care. Come right now if you can."

I laughed and said, "You've got to be kidding. Funny, Patrick!"

He told me he was serious but would not tell me what was going on. Incredulous and obviously concerned, I turned my car toward urgent care.

I met Patrick and his dad in the parking lot and immediately noticed the blood all over Patrick's arms and shirt, my eyes darting quickly to the blood-soaked towel he was holding to his face. What?! I just stared at him in disbelief. Apparently, between innings at the slow-pitch game, he and his dad were practicing fast pitches. His dad slung a ball at him when he looked away for a second, and WHAM, it hit him right between the eyes. My man had a shattered nose, multiple abrasions, and swollen, blackened eyes. Just the look we wanted for our wedding pictures. Ugh!

Urgent care stitched him up and said his nose would need surgery after our honeymoon once the swelling subsided. As we walked to the parking lot with his parents, I realized this would be a defining moment for us as a couple. Instead of returning to his childhood home with his parents, he headed for my car and my parents' house to receive the expert care he knew he would get as a result of my nursing training. I felt sad for his mom in that moment, but really, it was such a sign of independence and an indication that she had done her job well. He was in my care now, and that seemed right. We had a mere six days to get my man ready for our wedding, and despite the guilt Patrick's dad felt, I was determined to keep everyone focused on the wedding ahead and the healing I was sure would come. Everyone thought I would be angry, and I suppose I was for a flash, but it was such a disaster that all I could do was obsess over Patrick's healing and the tasks at hand. There really wasn't time to be angry; it was quite ridiculous!

Patrick literally sat in a recliner for six days, never lying down even to sleep. He followed my militant icing schedule for his purple, swollen eyes while doing all he could to help with last-minute details for the big day. It was a week we will never forget!

When we went to our pastor's office for the last counseling session of our premarital therapy, he outright laughed when we walked through the door. A week before, we had passionately disagreed while sitting on his couch, and now Patrick showed up with two black eyes, a bandaged nose, and a giggling fiancée! What a vision we were that week; good thing we decided we were not going to focus on perfection in our relationship!

Friday finally arrived, and the wedding rehearsal went well. Our family and friends enjoyed a lovely catered barbecue with all the fixings at my parents' house, and I tried to stay as calm as I could as I enjoyed our bridal party and families. I just kept glancing at my purple-eyed fiancé and wondering how he was going to look in the morning! My Aunt Catherine headed to Macy's late that night to gather some makeup for the camouflage job she hoped to accomplish before Patrick met me at the end of the aisle on Saturday. I carefully removed the stitches on Patrick's nose before he headed for our new apartment that evening. It would be his last night without me there.

The morning of the wedding, I felt mostly calm and collected. I went to get my hair styled by a professional but returned home to apply my own makeup and nail polish. I felt anxious to get to the church, to get the party started! Months of planning and a week of intimately caring for Patrick had me chomping at the bit to start my new role as his wife. I smiled all the way to the church.

My bridesmaids were upbeat, and laughter quickly filled the bridal suite. To add more fuel to the giggling, my Aunt Catherine marched in and announced that Patrick's makeup was complete; he looked great. We could not stop laughing; the groom's makeup was finished before the bride's face! In a quiet moment, she also gave me some great advice that morning, "Kacey, don't forget to take a moment and slow down and feel everything today: his tux, the smell of the flowers, the sounds of the music. It will all go so fast and you'll miss these things if you don't make a point to notice them." I'm so grateful she took the time to focus me before I walked out to meet my dad.

When I saw my dad standing there waiting to escort me down the aisle, I melted with such great love for him. What a special relationship we shared over the years. My eyes filled with tears to match his emotion, but we both pulled it together in time to take our proud march down the aisle, my bouquet of red and white roses gripped tightly in my free hand. I kept my eyes on Patrick the whole time and was deeply moved by the tears filling his eyes as well. Just like Aunt Catherine encouraged me to do, I savored the softly lit ceremony and even noticed the heavy weight of the fabric of Patrick's black tuxedo as we lit our unity candle together. I never felt like I was on a stage, which is exactly what I had hoped and planned for all those long months. My dream guy promised his life to me, and I promised him right back. The passionate kiss he planted on my lips made me weak in the knees, prompting me to grin at the audience after it was over, my head resting dizzily on his chest. I marched back down the aisle to roaring applause with a smile that lasted the rest of the day.

Our exit from the church was filled with a sea of bubbles blown at us by all our families and friends. We rode in a limo to Pinehurst Country Club with the bridal party after taking pictures at the church and signing our marriage license. Mr. and Mrs. Patrick Johnson! I loved writing my new name. While guests arrived for the reception, our photographer took Patrick and me out to the golf course for a private photo session. It was our favorite memory of the day, munching on snacks together and enjoying the beauty of the course, while striking romantic poses for photographs in the early evening light. My dad said it felt like forever waiting for us to arrive to the reception, but we didn't care. We were determined to enjoy every moment.

With my veil tucked away and my pretty up-do on display, we waltzed into the reception as husband and wife ready to party all night. My sister and Patrick's brother gave memorable toasts, and we enjoyed feeding our three-layer white cake to each other in between greeting each guest and dancing. Exhausted but relaxed, we were whisked away to the airport in a limousine to begin our honeymoon and our new life together as the reception ended. It marked the happiest day of my life thus far. I cried such happy tears that night, acutely aware of how hard the climb had been to such an incredible height. I intended to savor the view for a very long time.

CHAPTER 8

JUST ONE MORE

Watching the sun set on the sparkling Gulf of Mexico, my gorgeous husband lounging by my side, I had to pinch my bikini-clad body. Is this really my life? Sheer bliss. I really should live by a coast. I would take a sun dress and flip-flops over a ball gown and heels any day. The feel of the sand between my toes, the gentle crashing of waves on the shore, and the warm sun on my face are things I crave at a cellular level. It is such a calming experience for me, sitting on a beach, drinking in the beauty painted by a creative God. So much of my love story with Patrick was written on a beach, too. After such a big and eventful wedding week, the eleven days we spent in Playa del Carmen, Mexico, remain etched in our minds as some of the happiest, most carefree days of our lives. We did a lot of giggling over Patrick's still-black eyes as we ate and drank our way through the resort; I can only imagine what people must have thought about my husband! Although we were not sure why we called a landlocked state home, we returned to Denver tanned and refreshed, ready to embark on our life together as husband and wife. I felt healthier and more at peace than I had in a decade.

We jumped feet first into newly married life, quickly learning that individual decisions impacted the other person in significant ways. We studied this new dance together, and handled our disagreements with a lot of TLC early on. With Patrick running his painting business through word-of mouth referrals thanks to the excellence he brought to his job, I got to work right away as a cobreadwinner, supplying the health insurance we needed through my nursing job at Littleton Hospital. I couldn't wait to get to work; I finally felt great physically and enjoyed the opportunity to make a decent income. The seventh floor became my home away from home, and I was given four night shifts per week to start. Gazing at the view of the beautiful mountain vistas seen through the windows on the top floor would have to wait; something about the night shifts excited me and kept my mind laser-focused on my tasks. I would wake up at 4:00 p.m. to make dinner for my husband, then head to the hospital around 6:45 p.m.

Figuring out our new routine as a married couple was deeply satisfying; we got to see what worked for us, separate from our families of origin, but we used their examples as a framework. I loved building a new life with Patrick. Mundane tasks like grocery shopping and cleaning our bathroom felt like privileges. Not anymore, mind you, but young love makes you crazy! Many nights after my hospital patients were resting, Patrick would show up at the hospital around 10:00 p.m. with my favorite ice cream; we enjoyed spending time together during my short breaks.

The night shift offered me plenty of opportunity to get to know my patients. I was frequently found sitting by a patient's bedside, listening to them recount the upending moment they heard their cancer diagnosis, or about their subsequent battle with anxiety and fear as their treatment ensued, and their bodies began to rebel. It was such a privilege to get to share pieces of my own story to offer them hope; it was the best part about my job. I built trust quickly with my patients through our shared experience of physical difficulties and subsequent disabilities. I began to see the power of my story in the brightening of my patients' faces as I slowly revealed details about my life. If I could survive tragic, terrible things, so could they. We gathered strength from each other, and sometimes that strength required them to face death bravely. I got to stand beside many patients as they passed through death's door; I walked them to the finish line. Sometimes being brave means a patient gets to fight a disease and return to their life, stronger than ever. But sometimes disease doesn't give them a choice, and they get to decide how they're going to die. That year, I celebrated bravery in all its various forms on the seventh floor.

One night, I asked a patient, who was days away from passing, what she wanted to do with our night together. She said she wanted an ice cream party. After I settled my other patients into their beds for the night, the dear woman spent time making herself look pretty. When Patrick arrived with ice cream and a variety of toppings a little while later, the three of us had a little party I will remember forever. She couldn't stop smiling, and I think she took that smile to her grave.

The sacred moments of ushering great dignity into the experience of death for my patients gave my own suffering a new purpose. I was not afraid of pain. I felt equal joy watching a patient get to return home to their family after treatment. I truly cherished every facet of my intense work in the hospital, ever mindful of the great privilege I had been given.

Six months after our wedding, Patrick and I closed the door at our first apartment together and drove east to Parker where our first newly purchased home awaited us. Shortly after we moved in, we added two babies to our family: a yellow Labrador, Maggie, and a Golden Retriever, Penny. We had so much fun painting walls, fluffing dog beds, hanging draperies, choosing furniture, and carefully positioning art on our new walls. We loved our new life together; the waters were calm—finally. After about a year on the night shift, however, I was asked to move to the day shift. I begrudgingly left my night shift job behind, knowing that the day routine would be more conducive to stoking the fires of my marriage and seeing our friends and family. But I would miss the quiet time with my patients late at night. The day shift bustled with a different energy. But I was ready for the new challenge, and I jumped in, come what may.

The day shift was indeed different. I often clocked in at 7:00 a.m. only to feel like ten minutes had passed instead of a twelve-hour shift. There were some sacred moments sprinkled into my work, but mostly the new pace began to take its toll on my reconstructed shoulder. The greater demands on my body to lift patients began to weaken my surgical repairs. The pain increased daily, and after a year and a half on the day shift, my shoulder looked like it was dislocated. The pain became unbearable. I began to miss my shifts at the hospital, lying in bed instead. When I did show up for work, I often had to wipe tears off my cheeks after trying to lift a patient. Worried and scared, Patrick and I finally headed downtown to Dr. Wilkins's office.

"Kacey, I'm so sorry, but we need to preserve the work we have done on your shoulder. Assisting your patients on a daily basis is pushing it beyond its capabilities. Because we don't have a good option yet, I can't advise you to continue in your nursing career. We need to limit the use of your arm as much as possible." Dr. Wilkins's words felt like gunshots deflating the dream for which I had fought hard; I desperately wanted to continue in my nursing career.

I sat in disbelief while Patrick rubbed my back at the conference table. I could see the disappointment in Dr. Wilkins's eyes as well; he knew how hard I had worked, understood the sacrifices I had made. His bear hug at the end of my appointment helped soothe the pain of his pronouncement just a little, but I cried all the way home.

I decided to take a month off from my job, and wore a sling, hoping to give my shoulder some much-needed rest. Still, I needed heavy painkillers to make it through each day. At the end of the month, I was no better. I was in a heavy fog and growing increasingly depressed. Laying around and nursing my busted arm made my soul feel like winter again.

Noticing my tan, a well-meaning family member said at a gathering, "Hey, Kacey. Wow, it looks like you have been working hard!" I knew, of course, that she meant no harm and was trying to joke around with me. I even provided a quiet "Ha!" before leaving the table to gather myself. My internal turmoil continued to swirl as I thought, *Sure, maybe I am tan right now because all I can do is walk our dogs in the bright Colorado sun before heading back to the couch in pain each day, but I would never choose this routine.* My growing frustrations twisted her innocent observation into a diagnosis: I was broken beyond repair. The memories of the shooters and their sick game to destroy my life began to resurface, slowly ripping my beloved career and what was left of my self-esteem away from me. The depression sparked flashes of anger about my situation.

My month of rest gave Dr. Wilkins time to think. He believed it was in my best interest to be seen by another surgeon. The mechanisms that had been placed in my arm to hold it in the shoulder socket were stretched out due to the rigors of my job. The new idea was for a reverse shoulder, which is reserved for patients with a large rotator cuff tear where muscles no longer function. I certainly met the requirements. The reverse total shoulder replacement relies on the deltoid muscle, instead of the rotator cuff, to power and position the arm. After months of painful testing, it was determined that I lacked the necessary functional deltoid muscle to support the reverse shoulder surgery. I was devastated.

I cried every day in that low valley. Ripped from a job I loved and plopped on a couch with no sense of purpose, I longed for my shifts at the hospital. Instead, I was placed on long-term disability and faced with an uncertain future. I struggled with my identity: an arm that didn't function properly, no career, excessive pain, no kids, and seemingly no way out from underneath the heavy blanket of despair. Patrick felt helpless and my family worried I would sink into an even deeper depression. No one wanted me to start another fistfight with the hell I had already beaten down with all the grit I could muster for so many years. Did I have any grit left? No, I honestly did not: but my

God did. I would not walk this road alone. All would not be lost. A rescue was already in the works.

I had wanted to be a mother for as long as I could remember. The draw to motherhood was magnetic and I could think of little else. Even though Patrick wasn't quite ready for that next step in the life of our family, I downright begged him. And then begged him some more. I needed something positive and encouraging in my life, something to look forward to, and a new job. Eight long months and some medical intervention later, the pregnancy test finally showed two lines. We were ecstatic! Both of Patrick's siblings were already pregnant, which meant our kids would all be around the same age. The due date we were given was April 8; I breathed a sigh of relief that we had dodged April 20.

That year, my dad had been teaching a couples Bible study that Patrick and I attended together. At the class summer barbecue on my parents' property, Patrick and I handed my dad a thank-you note, but tucked inside was a picture from our first ultrasound of the baby. He opened the card, and stared blankly at the picture, not sure what he was seeing. But then, I started crying, and my mom looked over and knew exactly what the picture represented. Such rejoicing! It was a dream come true for me, giving the very first grandchild to my parents. True to my dad's dry sense of humor, he walked over to Patrick a few minutes later, patted him on the back and said, "But Patrick, I thought you told me you weren't going to touch her." *Dad!*

I went to the gym five days a week, ate and slept well, and had no nausea. As I watched my bump swell with each passing week, I was just plain giddy. The dark days of depression were waning, and then, after a while, they were no more. Onward and upward, rescued by the tiny life growing inside of me. We spent the next few months painting the nursery, celebrating the news that we were expecting a baby girl, and playing with different name options. I didn't enjoy gaining weight, but when I felt her move inside of me, all of that angst disappeared entirely. My depression had lifted and I got to thoroughly enjoy all of my pregnancy, anticipating my new role as a mother with great joy and fanfare.

I felt strong; all my daily exercise and good nutrition put a new spring in my step. A month before our baby was due, she dropped down low into my pelvis; I felt like I had a baby nearly hanging out of me all the time! But it was so nice to focus on a different part of my body than my shoulder. On April 1, a few days before my due date, we went to the doctor for a check-up. I was already six centimeters dilated and advised to return to the hospital early the next morning to meet our girl. We enjoyed a fun dinner out that night with Patrick's family and slept quite peacefully.

On the morning of April 2, 2008, the staff at Littleton Hospital broke my water and I was quickly in birthing transition, waves of powerful contractions racing through my body. Patrick was lying down on the couch in our room complaining of stomach pain while I was suffering in the bed. The nurses just thought he was anxious, but I was frustrated and angry with him. *Get over here and help me!* He was actually battling the stomach flu; it lasted our entire three-day hospital stay. Still, I did not entirely sympathize with him! After I pushed for a short ten minutes, I got to see Mallory Lynne's beautiful little face for the first time; I fell in love with her immediately. Her middle name is my mom's middle name, one I share with her as well. We carried her home with a deep sense of gratefulness. I was a mother; I felt something fierce awaken inside of me.

Mallory made us so proud. She slept through the night by seven weeks of age and was easy to schedule. I loved dressing her up and putting bows in her full head of hair. She even accompanied me to a small horse show I competed in when she was an infant; I borrowed a horse from my mom. It was an event I did not prepare for but enjoyed nonetheless. I did quite well, and I felt a flicker of the fire I used to feel for equestrian competition. However, I knew without a shadow of a doubt that horse competitions were not where I wanted to spend my time now. Mallory was my world and motherhood my new calling.

The physical demands of caring for a baby took their toll by the end of the summer, unfortunately. Rocking, cradling, nursing, and carrying Mallory's heavy car seat rendered my arm pretty useless. When Mallory was eight months old, I had a minor surgery to repair my shoulder socket, with strict instructions to rest both of my arms to allow my right arm to heal correctly. Yeah, right. I had a new baby, and nobody was taking her away from me. A month later, I had another minor surgery to fix another issue, and had to stay at my parents' home for a full two weeks to recover while accepting the help I needed to care for my baby. It was a humbling experience. Watching my parents as they comforted and diapered her frustrated me. I wondered if my shoulder would continue to get in the way of the mothering experience I craved. But I was dead set on not letting it rule my life, and I returned home two weeks later with my baby in tow.

Two months later, I was pregnant with baby number two. We were elated but surprised. Our children would only be seventeen months apart! I had a newly renovated arm and an easy baby by then, so I was undaunted by the thought of having two young children. Dreams were coming true! Like my first pregnancy, I felt great. The baby measured pretty small on a consistent basis, so we had a lot of extra testing to make sure everything was progressing well. Each time we heard "the baby is fine" after an ultrasound I could breathe a little easier. The second day of the month seems to be a recurrent theme in our family. Like her sister, Logan Jo arrived on September 2, 2009, at Littleton Hospital after an easy birth and uncomplicated hospital stay. Jo is Patrick's mother's middle name. However, unlike her quiet sister, Logan was screaming from the moment she arrived.

Long nights awaited us at home, to put it mildly. I can probably handle lack of sleep better than the next person, but night after night of not being able to comfort my screaming baby took its emotional toll. I would end up in tears, which forced me to trade places with Patrick; I needed to distance myself from the nearly constant noise so I could think clearly. Logan hated being outside, and long walks in the stroller were torture. She hated the car, too, which ruled out drives to get her quieted down. We battled her colic and reflux, both of us bleary-eyed, for months and months. It was utterly exhausting. Our easy experience with Mallory had led us to believe we were such good parents, but our inability to satisfy Logan quickly humbled us. No matter what, I was motivated to help my sweet baby push through her issues and find some peace, even though I wasn't sure what to do.

One fall day, Logan was sitting contentedly on my mom's lap at her house. My mom thought maybe some fresh air would be good for her, so she walked her out onto the porch as she sat perched on my mom's hip. Logan immediately began screaming, prompting my mom to casually mention that she must not like something outside. In the meantime, I began to notice that Logan wasn't meeting the regular infant milestones I had experienced with Mallory. Specifically, she never made eye contact with us, and that was really hard. Also, she was not connecting her hands at midline, or finding her feet with her hands. So, at an appointment for her ongoing reflux issues, on a whim, I asked the physician assistant to check Logan's eyes.

The PA shined a light into our daughter's dark eyes, raised her eyebrows, then stood up and said she would return to the exam room with a doctor. I tried not to panic. When the doctor returned, she said she immediately noticed a strange red reflex in our baby's eyes. Logan's eyes appeared almost black to us, which we always thought was interesting since Patrick has blue eyes and mine are green; most members of our families have light eyes. We had also noticed that Logan's eyes showed up red in every picture we took of her. The doctor suggested I take her to a pediatric ophthalmologist immediately. All alone with my racing thoughts, I put her in the car and drove straight to the eye specialist's office, shaking all the way there. I quickly let Patrick know what I was doing through choked sobs on the phone. I can hardly remember driving to the office; I was in such a daze. The staff ushered Logan and me back to an exam room right away.

Aniridia. Our daughter was born with aniridia. I would come to learn that it means the absence of an iris in the eyes. However, I quickly discovered that the missing iris was merely the definition of the word aniridia, not the all-encompassing diagnosis. I was told she would possibly be legally blind, never drive a car, and most likely suffer from significant related issues, potentially even malignant tumors in her kidneys. My innocent baby. Everything within me wanted to shield her from this diagnosis. I sat in stunned silence. The doctor told me not to look up anything online, knowing it would scare me. My nursing background provided me enough knowledge to ask important questions about potential needs, prevention of certain side effects, medications, treatments, etc. I started firing questions, lots of them; most of which he wouldn't answer. I think my emotional maternal response—fueled by my severe lack of sleep—made him uncomfortable; he seemed unsure about how to handle the situation. I left fuming and confused, fastening my precious girl in her car seat and dialing Patrick as soon as I started the drive home. I sobbed as I recounted the devastating news, and he started crying with me. The shock and grief cut us deeply. In a daze, we phoned our families and filled them in on Logan's difficult diagnosis. They all cried with us.

A daughter with disabilities? But I am a disabled mother! Are you kidding me, God? A person close to me even said, "Well, at least she doesn't have cancer, and she gets to live." Really? I had to work through my rage over that comment for years. *Walk a mile in my shoes,* I thought. I ached over my loss of a "healthy daughter" that day and began my slow journey to acceptance of a daughter with a disability. I would soon be her champion, but in the days after Logan's diagnosis, I needed to grieve.

I made a quick decision to find another physician. I knew we needed to build a long-term relationship with a doctor with whom we felt comfortable; someone with the patience to respond to long lists of questions. The next day, Logan and I returned to the same eye specialty clinic and were greeted by a female doctor who kindly allowed me to ask every question under the sun, responding with a calm confidence that soothed my fear. She made me feel safe while the ground beneath me rumbled, and I'm grateful for that time with her. I shot a lot of questions toward the sky, too, wondering what God had planned for our girl. I was never angry about her diagnosis, but I still had questions about how this particular plot line in my daughter's story would be *good* for my girl. She would never experience clear vision. My own personal suffering was easier to handle than the suffering of my child; I quickly learned this truth.

Aniridia, we soon found out, demanded special accommodations. The Anchor Center for Blind Children became a safe haven for our daughter. The place was an absolute godsend. Built with sensory issues in mind, there were bright colors, bold contrasts, and different textures of flooring to mark a new room or hallway. Braille, calming swings, and weighted blankets awaited Logan there. There was even a sensory garden outside with alternating paths of rocks, sand, dirt, water, and stones—just *amazing.*

We arrived at our first visit feeling broken and lost. Our sleep deprivation only worsened the situation. We had no idea how to help our baby. Mallory never cared how we rocked her, or about how dark or bright the room was when we fed her, but Logan sure did. From the very beginning, the staff was so gentle and encouraging. Never once did I feel ashamed of my tears or the myriad of questions I asked at each visit. They taught us things that first day that changed our lives immediately. We learned new ways to help Logan process the world around her. She felt completely out of control; she needed us to help her rein it all in. Like a strong horse with blinders on, she needed to learn the skills I had gathered for years in the showcase ring. I could do this. I *would* do this.

Patrick's mom, Marty, recalled the first time she went to the Anchor Center with me to see what they were doing for Logan there. She remembered watching me sit on the floor with our baby, listening to the therapist share her specific ideas. She ached as she watched me break down in sobs: sobs of relief. Qualified and trained staff knew how to help us meet the needs of our precious Logan Jo. The therapist met us on the floor and gave us building blocks of hope, blocks that would eventually build a strong and safe tower for our girl.

For the next eight months, Logan spent hours swaddled in her car seat with a weighted beanbag on her lap and a blanket cover draped over her to keep the light out. We ordered specialized infant sunglasses that she quickly learned to wear without a fight. Bright lights felt like fingernails on a chalkboard to her. They still do. When she looks at something, she sometimes sees a kaleidoscope of colors and lights, and has limited peripheral vision.

The staff helped us navigate through different motions that would not trigger Logan's sensitivities. Many babies with aniridia like swinging. Not Logan! She wanted to be in her car seat or wrapped tightly in a blanket and bounced. This was NOT good for my arm, but I had no choice, and I bounced that girl for hours. Every time she needed to nurse, I would have to find a dark and quiet room, often turning on a fan just to soothe her. We spent a lot of time in dark closets or bathrooms for that first year while she was nursing, and I was grateful to have a reprieve from the constant screaming she exhibited in the early months of her life.

It was a gift to us that Mallory was so easy, because Logan demanded a lot of extra time and energy to get her to a place of functioning well in our family environment and the community at large. We had to travel two days a week to the Anchor Center to work on occupational therapy (OT); we worked diligently on OT every day at home, too. It was exhausting, but also gratifying. Experts gave us the necessary tools we needed to reach our little girl in a way that resonated with her; we were finally able to provide her with a lifestyle that would allow her to grow, learn, and thrive.

It was clear we were living very different lives from parents with healthy children, but we slowly embraced our new normal. We spent more than two years attending the Anchor Center's therapies and classes. Logan caught up quickly. The more time we spent with her, teaching her how to navigate the world through the eyes she had been given, the more joyful and happy she became. Her smile always lit up the faces of her therapists at the center, and she continues to be a bright light in this world. She is thriving in every aspect of her life today with the help of trained eye specialists and educators, as well as the strength she gathers from the love of her family.

Only God could have known that the injuries I sustained at Columbine would turn into a huge blessing with regard to my parenting journey. I don't think anybody could have scripted that story back in the smoky haze of 1999. Knowing my Logan will have to adapt to different ways of functioning makes me thankful that I was chosen to be her mom. I get to be a living, daily witness of how wonderful life can be with a disability, that it only holds me back as far as I will let it. I can understand my daughter's physical struggles in ways few others can, and that gives beautiful purpose to our mother-daughter relationship. It is a sacred calling in my life that I don't take lightly. The hard-fought leadership I have in this regard has taken many years to develop; helping Logan navigate her struggles makes my journey worth it. Mostly, my heartfelt prayer and hope for Logan is that she uses her disabilities to encourage others—there is always a reason to hope and push for a brighter tomorrow. Step onto that stage and share your gifts with the world, girl!

After bringing our first two children into the world, we needed some time to recover. But we had always dreamed of building a large family together, so we pursued adoption a couple of years after Logan Jo was born. Two of the agencies where we applied rejected our applications because of my "disability." I did not understand how I could be considered an unfit mother for precious children needing a home; it took me a while to get over that rejection. Nevertheless, we became pregnant with our third child when Logan was two. My pregnancy was difficult for the first time, and I was an emotional wreck for nine long months. Because Logan screamed, kicked, and fought routine pressure checks of her eyes, ripping my heart out in the process, we had to spend a lot of grueling days at Children's Hospital with Logan under anesthesia to get accurate readings. These days took their toll on my pregnant body, and I fought emotional fatigue every day. Being at Children's provided us with a new perspective on Logan's diagnosis, however. We always left our appointments thankful that we were not required to live at the hospital like so many hurting families dealing with their children's life-threatening illnesses. We were in and out of the hospital for the most part; we had specialists battling on our daughter's team who always took the time to fill our tanks with hope. We stopped complaining pretty quickly.

I think my rough pregnancy rubbed off on our third daughter's personality. Bentley Mae was born on June 18, 2012, after another easy delivery. All blonde, fiery, and dramatic, she brought a sass to our family that had been missing. We began to worry that having three daughters so close together might make for an odd girl out situation. But no. "Benz" is a trailblazer in her own right, and is just fine being the boss of everyone and everything, thank you very much. Her place in the birth order doesn't hold her back, that's for sure. Patrick likes to remind me she is the only "Benz" I'm ever gonna have. The girl certainly lives up to her name; she is really high end!

We never wanted the names of our children to fall on the top one hundred baby names' list. I love unique names. I love that each of our children's names honors our family in some way. I spent months researching names for our third child. As I was looking through old family lists of names, one in particular stood out immediately. Bentley is the last name of my mom's family that came to America from England on the Mayflower, and Mae is the middle name of Patrick's maternal and paternal grandmothers. Bentley was actually born on my grandmother's birthday.

We settled into a new routine with three beautiful girls, thankful to have a successful game plan for Logan's eyes in place, and enjoyed the busyness that comes with trying to raise small children. Our family savored long walks to Starbucks, enjoying a treat or two, and spent long hours at parks and on the trails behind our home. The new rhythm of our lives felt really good, and we cherished it. Not too long after our season of peace started, Patrick brought up the idea of a fourth baby—a fourth girl, mind you, since we don't make boys. I just laughed at him and rolled my eyes.

In August 2013, we drove our girls to California for a vacation before school started. We drove all the way through the night. As we arrived in a small town in Nevada for breakfast, Patrick stayed in the car to take a quick nap. I took the three girls into McDonald's for breakfast. As I stood there ordering, suddenly, my blood pressure tanked, and I almost passed out. I knew what was happening; this was my telltale sign of pregnancy! After we ate, I loaded the kids in the car and quietly whispered to Patrick, "I think I'm pregnant."

He said, "Really?! YES!" I think I rolled my eyes again.

That evening, after checking into our condo, I took a pregnancy test before we went for a walk on the beach. It appeared to be negative at first glance. I thought to myself, *Hmmm . . . maybe it's just too early for a positive test.* When we returned from our long walk, I was sitting in the kitchen of the condo when Logan walked over to me, holding the pregnancy test she had found in the bathroom trash. As I snatched it away from her, annoyed and lecturing her about not touching the trash in the future, I noticed *a very faint second line.* We rushed out to the store for another test, and sure enough, the second one showed two very faint lines. It was the best way to start a vacation; we would be expecting one more little person at the family dinner table in about eight months! The thought crossed my mind about the physical impact of raising four children, and I wondered if caring for a fourth newborn would lead to another surgery. Nevertheless, I was excited.

I felt very different this time around, though. Sick. I couldn't stomach anything. Dizzy and exhausted. I've never been one to nap or lay around . . . I'm a total doer. It took all my effort just to drag myself off the couch. I barely made it through that week on the beach with my family and back to Colorado in the car.

With the girls' pregnancies, we had insurance that allowed us to choose a doctor. With that doctor, we were fortunate enough to get 3-D ultrasounds; the images were so clear. We changed insurance plans prior to getting pregnant the fourth time around. Our new doctor didn't offer the same quality ultrasounds, sadly. We went for my twenty-week check-up, secretly hopeful for a boy, but sure we were expecting a girl. But, in the back of our minds, we wondered why I had been feeling so terrible compared to the other pregnancies. The dark room got quiet as we waited for the ultrasound tech to make a pronouncement. "It's a BOY!" she exclaimed after a few long minutes. We were utterly shocked, and I'm pretty sure I laughed out loud. She then said, "Do you see that? If that isn't a baby boy, I don't know what is." The ultrasound was not all that clear to our untrained eyes, however. We left the office choosing to believe that we were expecting a boy, but for months I had dreams that the ultrasound was wrong.

We struggled to come up with a boy name. Choosing an uncommon girl name felt easier for some reason. Boy names all felt the same to me. We finally picked Corban Patrick, choosing a more unusual spelling because it changed the meaning. His name means "gift given to God." I spent the rest of my pregnancy doubting my parenting abilities; I didn't know what I was going to do with a boy! Granted, I love sports and prefer hanging with my brothers to fluffy girl chat and shopping, but we raise girls; babies are always *girls* at our house! I had no idea how I would handle having a boy. That is, until the moment he was born on April 18, 2014.

We've never looked back and continue to rejoice over the completion of our family; we have three unique girls and one hockey-stick-wielding wild man. I have four children that the shooters at Columbine never thought I would have; it is never lost on me, this miracle. Not a day goes by that I am not thankful for my mothering experience. Sometimes I see pictures of my family or watch the kids playing in the park and shake my head in disbelief. But I think my body has had enough reconfiguration to last seven lifetimes. My family of six feels just right.

CHAPTER 9

LETTING GO

*H*e parks his car quietly, unnoticed, opening his trunk discreetly in the sea of vehicles in the parking lot. He's been watching the building for a while now, and he knows when the security officer takes his break and what door is unlocked near the playground. He knows right where to go at this hour of the day, having rehearsed his plan hundreds of times in his mind, hell-bent on getting his revenge on a system that never included him. He's flippant this morning in his thoughts: these unsuspecting people deserve this pain. Today, he'll make them hurt as badly as he does.*

Cloaking his head in a dark sweatshirt, he walks with purpose to the unlocked door, slipping inside quietly and without incident, sensing he is somehow welcome, even. The cold metal gun hidden next to his chest fuels his confidence. The system will finally pay attention to him, after all this time; he will make sure of that. The line between the violent games he plays on his computer in his dark, cramped apartment and what he is about to do is very, very blurry. He does not care that he is confused and dizzy with adrenaline. He feels like he's floating, free from all consequences. Releasing this rage opens something locked deep inside of him. His mouth twists into a smile as he begins to execute his plan.

My Mallory is writing a creative paragraph in her classroom under the careful instruction of her teacher who is also a young mother of two. My girl is daydreaming as she chooses words and images to craft her masterpiece.

Logan is in the lunchroom with a gaggle of first graders, foraging through lunch boxes packed by mothers who wish their children were still innocent kindergartners, sitting at home in their onesie pajamas at the kitchen counter at noon.

Bentley is coloring in her preschool room, surely bossing somebody around, shaking her blonde hair this way and that, making her mark. My friends' children roam the hallways; there are kids piled on beanbags in the library, too, absorbing books like little sponges. My neighbor's twins are in the business tech room, learning how to type. Someone very young is singing on key in the music room, and the teacher is smiling as the notes ring out, so pure, angelic even. The noise from the rowdy game of dodgeball being played in the gym echoes through the hallways; the teacher's whistle punctuating the children's happy shrieks.

He is next to the preschool classrooms now, and the front desk administrator quickly notices him on the security monitor at her desk. Her heart stops. Her hands are shaking as she sounds the alarm, discordant sounds flying through classroom speakers, and her fingers fumble on the keypad on the phone as she instinctively tries to reach the authorities through the officer in the building who is on break eating his lunch. But it's too late. The cloaked man pulls his weapon out of his shirt and opens fire. The alarms are sounding now, and heroic teachers are racing to lock flimsy doors and lower worthless paper blinds, shepherding children into dark corners, but it's all just too late. Lives are being snatched. Innocence is being stripped away. Floors are covered in blood. Young ears are absorbing sounds they were not meant to hear. A hastily typed alert is flashing on the screen of my cell phone. BUT I AM STUCK AT HOME. Powerless to do anything to save my girls.

I wake up, sobbing. And sometimes, I don't even have to wake up, because this is how my mind wanders unchecked during the day. The fear about sending my kids to school is the greatest fear I face; to this day, it is my greatest fear.

My "practice" for sending my kids to school started when Mallory was just a baby. I refused to leave her in any church nursery that did not have a secure room, and

I demanded a thorough inspection before I could hand her over to someone else's care. As the years ticked by and nothing significant happened, I slowly relaxed and enjoyed the worship and sermons I so desperately needed as a tired mother with young children. God worked on my fears in church, slowly but surely, and Patrick and my parents were also a great help to me in this regard.

When it came time to consider preschool for our firstborn, I agonized over the decision. The homeschool option appealed to me the most, as I wanted to be with my children all day, every day to make sure they were protected from all danger. I did not necessarily have a passion for teaching them, though, and I knew I needed to pay attention to that. I knew the pros and cons of homeschooling, but in my heart, I unequivocally believed there were better and more equipped teachers in the world. I didn't want my fear to handicap my kids' scholastic experiences. But it was like pulling teeth, getting me to consider traditional school. I fought it hard. I didn't want to let my kids be subjected to the vulnerability I experienced in the Columbine library years earlier. Sending my kids to school felt like I was saying to the world, "Here are my kids. Go ahead, shoot them." When the unthinkable happens, it is no longer unthinkable. It becomes what is expected instead. Never mind that my kids were more likely to be hurt in a car accident or by falling off playground equipment than being shot in a school, but the fear was real for me.

I settled on a private preschool for Mallory's first year. I inspected the building and met with staff and teachers, so they could give me their assurances about the security of the facility. I needed to hear details about their security plan; I wanted to know how the school planned to react to a perceived threat. Would the kids be on lockdown? Would they be told to run? And how did they plan to communicate with parents in the event of an emergency? On the first day I left Mallory in her new classroom, I trudged out to my minivan and cried all the way home. It was a mixture of happy and sad tears, and I felt somewhat triumphant, but not in a truly satisfying way. I had to fight off all the disturbing images in my head as I drove away. What we ultimately found, though, was that Mallory blossomed out in the world away from the comfort of our family, as she slowly gathered new social skills and showcased her remarkable academic strengths. Mallory's confidence grew in ways I couldn't have predicted when I ran her life 24/7. School was a new and exciting place for her to shine. However, it became clear to Patrick and me that affording private school for all our children was going to be impossible with our income. We needed an alternative.

We wanted to find a school that felt smaller and more intimate than the large public school located a block from our house. While the ease and familiarity of that choice would have made our lives much simpler, I knew it wasn't the right school for our family. I wanted my kids to be fully known by a smaller staff, and to have a school experience that would build upon the values we taught our kids at home. We settled on a charter school called SkyView Academy, about a fifteen-minute drive from our house.

A dear friend was already sending her children there, and I loved her kids and what they had already grown to stand for in their young lives; it was clear the school celebrated and encouraged the growth of the whole child, not just their test scores and academic achievements. The school implemented a strict dress code of uniforms and enforced rigorous discipline policies. I attended every meeting I could and signed my girls up for preschool, knowing that would help them get off the very long waiting list for kindergarten. The fenced-in playground felt like an added bonus to allay my ever-present fears, and clocking in the required forty hours of volunteer time per year felt like a safety measure to me. The eyes and expertise of hundreds of parents would continually be cast over my children, paired with the leadership of many excellent teachers and staff. We enrolled with wholehearted enthusiasm.

My fears sat in the front seat next to me on the way to school every day, though, whispering their lies. It was a daily fight. I slowly began telling parts of my story to my children's teachers in an effort to help them understand why I picked up my kids a bit teary-eyed a lot of afternoons. Saying goodbye to my girls became a disciplined exercise in self-restraint every morning, my smile forced. But my desire to keep the girls safely tucked under my wings slowly diminished as each day proved more and more successful. I was determined not to let my issues color their school experiences, even though I warned the teachers that I might show up at some point and usher my kids out of the building if something frightened me in the local news. My children were thriving, though; it was obvious to everyone. Patrick and I were thankful for the positive experience.

That is, until December 14, 2014. The Sandy Hook school shooting.

Patrick was in California with his brother on a vacation I gave him for his birthday. He desperately needed the time away, and I was glad to send him off. I was planning to leave that day with Mallory for afternoon kindergarten, dropping Logan at SkyView's preschool before returning home. As I was about to make them lunch before leaving for school, I flipped on the news. I dropped to my knees in front of the television. My very worst nightmare had come true. Children, the same ages as mine. This was really happening. We were just kids at Columbine all those years ago, but these were *babies*. All I could think about were *my* babies as I watched the frantic adults scrambling to help the kids on my TV screen. Unbelievable . . . yet believable. My heart started pounding wildly in my chest. I worried my entire chest might unzip and all the life would just spill right out of me.

I got nauseous and could not function normally; I started to hyperventilate. I called Patrick in a panic. I immediately went back to where I was thirteen years ago. I was suddenly that seventeen-year-old girl who could not leave my house. I could not take care of my kids. My husband wasn't home to help me. I quickly decided that my girls were not going to school that afternoon. Maybe *never again*.

Within a couple hours of the tragedy, news stations were calling to seek my "expert" opinion. Their approach angered me, and I thought to myself, *Being a survivor of a school shooting makes me an expert on exactly nothing*! I obliged one of the requests, but instead of sharing anything eloquent, I only spoke words of shared sorrow as tears streamed down my cheeks. My PTSD hit me hard; I became paralyzed with fear. I could not leave my house for two days. Patrick and my parents quickly became worried about how much I regressed; my reaction to this event scared them. That night, my dad drove to our house where he set up watch on our family room couch. At my strong request, he brought his concealed gun which remained by his side. He, of course, came to calm my fears; my family was not in any real danger. The next day, my mom came over to watch the kids while Dad took me to the grocery store. It was a short venture into the world to attempt to overcome my fears. I begged my mom to keep the kids inside the house while I was away.

It was a terribly violent battle between the two worlds that existed in my mind. My victimized world was in control, but my healed and healthy world was fighting for its life. It was exhausting; I was furious with the amount of control Columbine still had over my mind, coaxing the victimized side of my brain to take over and wreck all the progress I had made. Over the next few days, with all the energy I could muster, I was set on helping the healthy side of my mind take control again. I would win this one; with God's help, I would.

I didn't totally understand how it was going to happen, but I knew that I was not going to waste thirteen years of hard-fought healing. This was a moment—if I could just be brave enough to accept it—that I knew God had more healing to offer me. It could be groundbreaking for my journey going forward. I remember laying on our bed one afternoon a couple of days after Sandy Hook as all the kids napped; I was on the phone with Patrick who was still stuck in California. He had offered to fly home, but I didn't want my fears to ruin his vacation. We tried to figure out how I would get our girls back to school. SkyView Academy had assured me the kids could miss as much time as I needed. But I knew that this fear had no place in my life, at least not a place with so much power. I was giving power to all the fear, and that made me feel so weak.

Patrick tried to give me a helpful tool as we talked. He suggested, "Kace, when you feel afraid, clean out the closets or do laundry or distract yourself somehow." It wasn't a bad idea, but right away I knew distracting myself was only a Band-Aid. It wasn't the fix I needed. It was the easy way out, and I could not afford more distractions to bandage my problems. Up until that moment of realization, the visuals I always reverted to—blood, gunpowder, death, injury, pain, fear—were all that I allowed to fill my mind in moments of feeling exposed or afraid. But, in that moment with Patrick on the phone, I realized, the same Hand upon my back in my time of unbearable distress was available for my kids, too. As the popular songwriter Chris Tomlin's song says, *The God of angel armies is always by my side. Whom shall I fear?* I clung to those lyrics and blasted the song in my minivan every chance I got. The truth was that I was never left alone at Columbine. My kids would never be left alone, either, no matter what was headed their way. God's presence would never leave them.

If there is a gift my life could offer, it would be that one moment of feeling the Hand on my back, and helping others to realize it exists for them, too, in all of life's guaranteed heartaches and miseries. People can debate theology all day long, but it is hard for me to refute the power of God manifested in my life. It is a lifelong reminder of God's very real presence in my life. From that day on the phone with Patrick until now, every single day I drive my kids to school, I pray over them and with them. I pray over the school and all who enter it. And, instead of the terrifying visuals my mind tries to offer, I choose the visual of my Jesus with his angel armies standing guard over my children. I'm so grateful for compassionate educators the whole world over who work with parents to maximize children's school experiences no matter the family's background. Our family has been the recipient of so much attentive kindness.

It is a daily choice to dig deeply and find the bravery buried deep inside of me to send my kids to school. It is still terrifying sometimes, given all of the recent news in our country. I leave the school in tears occasionally. And when I pick up my kids, I often cry quietly to myself on the way home; the tears represent my gratitude for the blessing of bringing my kids home with me, as I'm uniquely aware of the alternative. I may not always think the right thoughts each day, but I'm determined to rise above challenges for the greater good of those I love.

I trust that my kids will learn more from my jump over this "going to school" hurdle than from the physical disabilities I have overcome. I am not a hero because I survived the Columbine shooting; but I would like to be a hero in my children's eyes because I choose, with God's strength, to go against my instinct to cower and hide for the rest of my life. This newfound bravery feels like a brightly wrapped gift. Maybe this gift can be used to shine some light and provide hope for others. My phone is about to ring, giving me the opportunity to share my newfound bravery. I'm shocked at how ready I am to answer the call.

CHAPTER 10

BEAUTY FROM ASHES

*E*ven *though it is a rainy and cold September day in
the beautifully nestled mountain town of Keystone,
Colorado, I can feel the sweat dripping down the back of
my dress like it's a hot summer's day in the deep South.
I'm waiting for Dr. Wilkins to finish his speech about the
importance of tissue donation, and I can barely hear him
through the loud drumming of my heart in my ears. He is
recounting the details of my unusual medical case to the
crowd, and I can see the mangled mess of my shoulder
and right hand on the X-rays being projected on the giant
screen behind him.*

*I'm secretly wishing I could just disappear and make
all of this go away. I am pretty sure I can't live up to what
Dr. Wilkins has requested of me this morning, certainly
not in front of this professional American Association of*

Tissue Banks crowd. I'm a nursing mother, for crying out loud, and certainly not a keynote speaker. What if my baby starts crying in the back of the room? What if my sleep deprivation makes me stumble over my words like an idiot? What if my emotions embarrass me, rendering me a blubbering mess in front of all these people? I definitely do not want their pity, and I can feel my defenses going up already. What if my message fails to resonate with anyone? My private nature drapes like a dark veil over my confidence. The last time I slept really well was about two days ago, and the exhaustion isn't helping my nerves. I'm pretty sure I'm going to throw up right here at the table. What a class act I am!

"And now, I'd like to introduce you to Kacey Ruegsegger Johnson, a young married mother of three who found herself on the floor of the Columbine library thirteen years ago, her body rearranged by a cowardly gunman. In desperate need, she had very limited surgical options when we first met in the hospital. Since then, I have watched her transform into the picture of health and vitality. She has become one of my favorite patients of all time and a good personal friend. She's here to tell you her story in her own words for the very first time."

I hear the applause as I float to the stage, utterly terrified. Dr. Wilkins embraces my shaking body before heading back to his seat. I can see Patrick smiling at me as he cradles our quiet newborn. I stare out into the sea of faces in the darkness below me, determined to make eye contact with my audience, and literally have to will my mouth to move. As the words spill out, I feel the tears sting my eyes immediately, tears springing from a deep well of fear, surprisingly not from sadness or emotion. I press on and continue talking.

As soon as I finish with a fifteen-minute version of my life story, I see hundreds of people rising to their feet. A standing ovation. I can't believe it, and my tears reappear, this time from relief and gratefulness. As soon as I make it to my seat in one piece, Patrick proudly throws his arm around me and Dr. Wilkins leans over and says, "I knew you could do it. But I loved watching your hands shake!" I crumple into Patrick's strong embrace, so thankful my time on stage is over. I can feel the adrenaline racing through my body. I look around and realize that my story has genuinely moved this crowd. Like, REALLY moved them; I did not expect this.

Without any warning, Dr. Wilkins heads back to the stage and opens up the microphones for questions, aimed at me! Reluctantly, I trudge back up to the stage. I have no idea how I can contribute to this professional discussion. A question quickly catches me off guard. "Do you in any way feel like the bones that were donated for your shoulder and hand reconstructions saved your life?"

I am too emotional to answer in the moment, so Dr. Wilkins jumps in and answers for me. "No, the donations didn't save her life. But they saved the quality of her life. She has two arms and two hands to ride her horse, wrap around her babies, and that make her morning runs on the trail balanced. It most certainly changed the quality of her life and her family's future. Our team is incredibly grateful for the gift of tissue donation in this case."

I nod in agreement, but I will ponder that question for a long time. Did the bone donations save my life? Soon, Dr. Wilkins concludes the session and I find myself at the head of a long line of well-wishing medical professionals. People seem genuinely thankful for my willingness to share my story; I hear them testify about other stories of loss and then tremendous gain, stories impacted directly by the gift of tissue donation. The crowd lets me know how my story gives great purpose to their tireless work. And I realize something: all the misery I endured and the anxiety which choked me as I prepared for my big speech is all worth it. It has truly encouraged people, and I feel a tiny fire light in my belly to do more. But just not today, please! I'm exhausted.

Yesterday, on the long and winding drive from Denver up to Keystone, Patrick received a call from Donor Alliance where he works. After the Rose Parade, Patrick hoped to become a firefighter. Instead, when he attained his EMT certificate, a job opened for him at Donor Alliance. He started as a Tissue Recovery Technician before moving to a new position helping to coordinate the donation process with families, hospitals, and processors. His interest in that position was directly related to my experience as a recipient. The Donor Alliance staff called Patrick and requested that I give a speech detailing my story at one of their upcoming large events. And yesterday, I told them no. But today? Today something is different, but I can't respond quite yet. This is all so overwhelming.

To get a break from my frazzled nerves, Patrick and I go for a walk with Bentley around picturesque Lake Dillon, hugged on all sides by the majestic Rocky Mountains. I always feel the power of God in the high country, and today is no different. Our phone rings while we are walking; it is the Limb Preservation Foundation calling, asking if I will consider keynote speaking at their annual fundraising breakfast the following month. Two more requests to speak within a day?

It took me two weeks to calm down from the event in Keystone. In the meantime, though, I shared a bit of what I was feeling with Patrick's brother, making it clear to him that God must be mistaken thinking that little, private me could be used in this capacity. He responded quickly, "Kace, I think you should start preparing yourself for how God is going to use you for His glory in ways that make you the most uncomfortable. Your weakness showcases God's strength in you. There's a lot of power in that." I pondered those comments for weeks before slowly believing the strong message.

I had spent a lot of time going back and forth about whether or not I should agree to my first keynote speech in Keystone; I'm so glad that I finally agreed to the invitation.

It revealed an opportunity for my story to be stitched with greater purpose and far-reaching impact. Initially, I spoke at that event for Dr. Wilkins, as a small way to thank him for all he had done for me. But I think he knew a doorway for my story existed; I only needed to experience it once to feel the power in it. A few weeks later, I accepted the two speaking requests I got that weekend, albeit somewhat reluctantly.

In the early years following the Columbine shooting, I had participated in some small speaking opportunities but nothing that resembled a keynote address. The multiple requests to give interviews for print magazines and news outlets continued for many years: I never liked any of that mostly due to audience response. I did not enjoy the feeling of pity I sensed from people. I have never lived life looking for pity, and that's probably why I have not written a book until now; I needed to be far enough removed from the actual life-changing event to keep that out of the audience's reaction to my story. Too many good things have happened, and I am thankful for the new responses to my story. The more I spoke, the more I got the sense that what my brother-in-law had said was in fact quite true: "Your weakness showcases God's strength in you." I became determined to let Him use my weaknesses for the greater good.

Many years earlier, God began to lay the foundation for sharing my story in public. One of the more significant speaking opportunities I was offered came on the heels of the horrific Virginia Tech (VT) shooting. I was asked to fly to Virginia with Philip Yancey, a brilliant and popular Christian author and speaker. He asked me to speak at a church service for the community, as well as participate in a question-and-answer session to offer my perspective as a survivor of a similar experience. VT was the next big shooting after Columbine; it happened on April 16, 2007, falling very close to the anniversary of the Columbine event.

I was terrified, but it felt right to be in Virginia, too. Traumatized people had just joined the club that nobody ever signs up for, and I was thankful to have the opportunity to be fully present, providing a fellow club member's honest, yet hopeful experience. All was NOT lost; I would try to make sure they understood that. Sure enough, though, my ever-present survivor's guilt began to surface as I listened to the VT survivors' stories. The beautiful people taken on that fateful day were stripped of their lives and the choice to create a loving family with four children, a choice I had been given. They would never compete or contribute in ways they would choose, ever again. It made me so incredibly sad; I had to wage a mental battle with my guilt.

That Sunday morning, we attended the church service that was also broadcast online. My dad remembers about one thousand students in attendance; he shared our story about Columbine, as I wasn't ready to speak to such a big group at the time. We stayed on the stage to field questions from the audience. One person asked me about survivor's guilt; he somehow felt guilty for not experiencing what some of his fellow classmates had endured. I addressed those who weren't there at the time of the shooting, talking about how the victims can often feel lonely and unheard in groups of people who don't share their tragic encounter with premeditated violence. I hoped my years of experience would somehow accelerate their healing process and bridge some painful gaps. Nevertheless, I went home with a heavy heart.

Despite lingering doubts and fear after my initial keynote in Keystone, a few short months later I honored my commitment to speak at The Limb Preservation Foundation (LPF). I had known about Dr. Wilkins's work with LPF for many years. The Foundation made a big difference for people like me who were at risk of losing an arm or a leg. I felt excited to share my story; I was still nervous and shaky, but I didn't cry as much as I had in Keystone. I was told later that my story offered hope to the doctors performing these limb-saving surgeries, as well as to the families and patients who were facing similar struggles.

Something happened after my presentation that October that had a significant impact on me. In the line of people waiting to talk to me was a twelve-year-old boy named Hunter. He shared with me that he had osteosarcoma in his leg; the doctors associated with LPF saved his leg with an allograft bone. But now, the cancer had returned and settled inside his lung. He was scheduled to have surgery the following Tuesday. He asked me to come and see him after the surgery. I quickly agreed to the visit.

I felt my nursing career rush right back to me in the hospital with Hunter that day. This new relationship aligned with one of my life's strongest passions: bedside care of patients and their families. Even though I could no longer do my job in an official capacity, I felt like God carved out special bedside time with Hunter for me. I spent two hours with Hunter and his parents; they poured their aching hearts out to me. My openness about my own suffering seemed to lift the floodgates on their emotions. Their heartache felt so holy to me, their words so sacred, and I held all of it in my heart. I listened intently, wiping my own tears away as I learned the details about the heavy weight of Hunter's incredible suffering.

After that initial visit with Hunter in 2012, I asked to be a volunteer for LPF. I joined the Patient Assistance committee, and soon thereafter was invited to join the Board of Directors. As a current member of this team, I have the opportunity to help create ideas and plans to assist patients and families experiencing very difficult circumstances with regard to limb preservation. I implemented the Patient Care Program which sends volunteers to spend time with patients during their hospital stays. Most of the volunteers serving in this program are previous patients who are looking for ways to give back. My work there brings me great joy.

As time passed, Hunter and I often exchanged text messages and emails. In the summer of 2014, I happened to run into Hunter, his dad, and older brother at Chipotle. I knew who he was right away; his smile was so recognizable. He certainly didn't look like the same Hunter who shyly approached me that first morning we met. He was so sick: pale, gaunt, and weak. Yet despite the physical obstacles laid in his path, he was as happy as any person in the restaurant, his laugh louder than the music playing on the speakers. I knew from conversations with his dad that Hunter was ready for the fight to be over; he had told his parents he wanted to be free. That day, his dad had taken him and his brother to have some fun at Cabela's, combing through the racks of their favorite fishing gear, before arriving at Chipotle for lunch. It was just enough activity for Hunter to enjoy before becoming too exhausted from his illness. He hugged me and asked more about me than he would reveal about himself, true to form.

Hunter was the perfect picture of courage, bravery, and abiding peace. More often than not, precious sick children are able to reach an unimaginable place of internal peace, despite their circumstances. He put up such a good fight. But at a certain point, he felt ready to lay down his armor and rest. And though his parents would have fought for him forever, they hugged him and said, "Okay, son. We understand." They spent their last months together soaking up family time. They went on short vacations;

his dad took many days off work, not wanting to miss a single moment with his son.

Then came the fateful weekend when I got a text from his dad letting me know the time had come. I knew exactly what he meant. In fact, just a day before, I had gotten a feeling that I would receive a message about Hunter and had even told Patrick quietly, "Hunter is almost free." The next text came in the very early hours of a Sunday morning in October 2014: "Kacey, he's finally free."

I can't explain why Hunter and I felt so connected; I felt it was a gift from God to both of us. Hunter offered me another perspective, even greater than the one I had already earned. He found joy in tragedy, and perhaps that great mystery is proof of the existence of God. His response to suffering was countercultural, too. Hunter lived his last two years the same way I hope to live my life, as a victor and not a victim. Cancer did not define Hunter. A young man with a vibrant faith, he never gave his illness control of his heart, mind, or spirit. He even requested that the focal point of his funeral would be the presentation of the message of Jesus. His memorial was a beautiful tribute to a life well-lived, and to the God he loved so much.

My two-year relationship with Hunter heightened my awareness of the importance of allowing grand purposes to sprout up from the often harsh ground of our stories; ultimately, keeping those details private steals the power they have to change other people's perspectives about their own difficulties. Despite his acute suffering, Hunter maintained an amazing sense of humor, bravery, and an always bright smile. He taught so many people how to truly live with gritty grace. His joy remains an inspiration to me.

As the months after Hunter's funeral ticked off the calendar, I began to really believe that sharing my story with people could make a real difference. When I was vulnerable, others could potentially be inspired to tackle their own mountains. I was ready to learn how to shelve my shyness for the sake of helping as many people as possible. The speaking opportunities began to pile up: Can you speak to our MOPS (Mothers of Preschoolers) group at church? Can you meet one-on-one with a teenage girl who is suicidal? Can you mentor victims from the theater shooting in Aurora, Colorado? Would you be willing to meet with troubled teenage boys who are incarcerated?

I remember one occasion when I was asked to fly to Arizona to speak at a conference about tissue donation. As I was checking in at the airport, I started to feel frustrated and angry with myself for agreeing to the request. Flying was not exactly my favorite activity, and the tight quarters often frightened me. Leaving my children behind was new to me, too; I felt incredibly guilty about it. Negative thoughts and emotions swirled inside me as I waited to board the plane. Yet, I was aware that there are very distinct times in my life when it becomes clear I am in the right place at just the right time, and I am usually out of my comfort zone when it happens.

The woman next to me on the plane started to engage me in conversation. I usually prefer to keep to myself and watch a movie when I'm flying, but she was friendly and engaging. I hoped the conversation would help the time pass quickly. As we talked, she started to reveal that she was having a lot of trouble with her teenage son. He was depressed, isolated, emotionally unstable, and she feared he would become suicidal. She eventually started to cry; her heartbreak on full display. I listened quietly, nodding my head in understanding. She took a pause and tried to pull herself together, so I decided to speak. I told her all about my high school years, my suicidal moments, my parents' constant pursuit of me in their battle to help me recover, and all that had happened since that tumultuous time. Listening to my broken story seemed to calm her down. And, the perspective I had as a teenager helped her see her own son's perspective on the situation. I suggested ways to reach out to him; the ways in which my parents and youth group leaders had reached out to me. Her body language slowly began to change, and she started to ask harder questions. I gave her honest and open answers about everything in my story, with the hope that it could somehow help her reach the heart of her son. When we landed and stood to exit the plane, the woman gave me a surprising hug. She thanked me for giving her hope, saying she believed she found new ways to connect with and understand her boy. I wished her well.

The reason I thought I was going to Arizona was perhaps not the reason I went at all. I stepped off that airplane reassured and confident that I absolutely needed to be away from my kids in that moment. I had been clearly put into a position to help someone else. That opened my mind and heart to the idea that each time I allow myself to be pulled away from my children, I can perhaps be used to impact another life.

Of course, I weigh each request carefully against my family commitments. The more I share, though, the more I feel like all this suffering I have endured has purpose beyond just the positive alterations in my own life. It also disrupts the ultimate plan the Columbine shooters had to submerge our community in lasting evil and hatred. All I have to do is be willing to give my story away to others. I have seen enough now to know that none of this is about ME; this isn't MY story. This is the story entrusted to me to use for a purpose far greater than I can imagine; I believe that with all my heart.

Perhaps the thing I hear the most from various audiences is exactly what they were doing when Columbine happened. It carried that kind of weight in their memories. Columbine made normal parents scared to take their children to school; it was an event that proved evil could and would cross unimaginable boundaries. It was a horrible moment in time that subsequently modernized school and childcare safety protocols. It never bothers me to hear the audience's stories. I enjoy the tender moments they share with me; they broaden my growing appreciation for good stories that remain untold.

Part of my inspiration has always been the precious family whose daughter was a donor for my shoulder. On April 20, 1999, my family was mere minutes away from deciding if I would be a donor. My donor family made a sacrifice in their darkest hours that forever altered the way I would get to approach my life. They made dreams possible that would have been otherwise impossible for me. A physical piece of someone else's life continues its journey in me; I'm so honored to live each day in appreciation for it. I have made efforts to reach out to my donor's family, but they have not responded. I hope that one day, they are able to learn how their selfless decision to donate has impacted my life and the people who love me.

One afternoon, I had given a presentation in front of a laid-back group of forty people at AlloSource. Shortly afterward, as I was enjoying conversations with Dr. Wilkins and my dad, a man who had clearly been weeping, approached me. Without a word, he reached out to hug me; it was a hug that lasted several minutes. His tears soaked through my shirt. He finally pulled himself together enough to step back and tell me the reason for his outpouring of emotion. He had recently lost his son rather unexpectedly; a young man with a bright future. As he and his wife said their painful goodbyes to him, they made the decision to donate his tissues. They learned that several people had been given the gift of his tissue donations, but they had not yet had the privilege of meeting a recipient. For this grieving father, I quickly became the face of their decision. He made it clear that my story gave such great purpose to his loss, knowing that a person like me was enjoying life because of his son. I felt incredibly humbled by his heartfelt transparency.

Moments like that one led me to ask myself, "How am I continuing to honor my donor and her family? How can I be sure the world knows about the possibilities? How can I help bring hope to families who lose their loved ones?" The allograft gift is not just a gift to the recipient; the gift is for the grieving family, too. The donation is never taken lightly or without high regard for the sacrifices involved. Telling my story hopefully continues the legacy of my donor, a daughter who meant the world to her grieving family; their brave gift providing me with an arm that has cradled all four of my babies. To me, tissue donation (like organ donation) is life-saving because it is so life-altering for struggling recipients. Quality of life can lead to unexpected and treasured quantity of life; I stand as a witness.

The more time I have spent with AlloSource, speaking on their behalf, the more I realized their mission fit right into what my life is all about. The gifts they facilitated for me—the donation of the bones used to repair my right arm and hand—have helped to provide me with a new life. I am reminded daily what a privilege it is to be alive, to have two arms and hands. My long healing process has led to a passion for meeting others in hard places, and subsequently I am learning how to use my story for the greater good. This new life I am leading is indeed richer than I could ever have imagined.

Now, six years after that shaky speech in Keystone, I feel comfortable in front of an audience. Nevertheless, I sometimes find myself whispering in front of the mirror, "I am a public speaker. I am a public speaker." I still struggle to believe it at times. I know I might be at the podium to touch just one heart with compassion or encourage one hurting person who desperately needs a message of hope. Or, I might even be up front to convince a family to choose to donate the tissues of a loved one when that difficult day comes. I also try to offer encouragement to anyone struggling with bitterness, who might feel like their broken story will never lead to anything good. I understand that struggle, but I truly believe anything is possible now. I've seen and experienced too much to believe otherwise.

For many years, I have been told, "You should write a book, girl." In response, I have always outright laughed at people. My little life seemed too bland, too blah, and too quiet. But the more I shared my story publicly, the more I realized that our world is craving hope; people often say that hope is the theme that comes through most clearly in my story. Our world seems desperate to understand how devastating situations can bring about any good, any good at all. I think the theme in my story unlocks some of that mystery. I am genuinely committed to creating beauty from ashes, no matter the cost.

We all have a powerful story worth telling, and this one is mine. I've embraced and championed the idea that every life has worth and value, no matter the dark pitfalls, and we do a great service to society at large by allowing others to learn from the broken tales we tell, perhaps gaining strength for their own battles in the process.

No difficulty gets wasted; this I know.

CHAPTER 11

OVER MY SHOULDER

I'm a little bit like Humpty Dumpty these days. My surgery count is at twelve and rising. Some parts of my body may always look cut and pasted in an odd array of unnatural shapes, and that's just how it is going to be; I have made my peace with it. But thanks to modern medicine and trailblazing doctors, unlike poor Humpty Dumpty, my mismatched body parts mostly work together! Recently, I sat in a sixth (yes, sixth) hand surgeon's office to discuss possible repairs for my hand that has increasingly demanded my attention with every tiny movement. Over time, the deterioration of the bones and tendons they used to repair it has caused a collapse of the joint at the base of my thumb. Decreased range of motion, grinding of bones, swelling, tendinitis, and pain are daily realities. The prescreening went a little like this:

"What was the date and time of your injury?" "Um, 11:32 on April 20, 1999."

This fact-finding nurse had no idea how weird this was about to get. "Um okay, what were you doing when the injury occurred, Kacey?" "Hiding under a table."

"What? Why?"

"Gunmen were going to shoot me."

Her mouth dropped open a little. I tried not to laugh inappropriately. "So how did the injury occur?"

"I was shot."

She stared at me for a moment to see if I was joking. "Huh, really? Okay, wow. Could you excuse me while I go get the doctor?"

Even I can't believe it sometimes, when I really think about everything that has happened to me. I certainly don't mean to make light of it, but my story often catches people off guard because it is so unexpected. Honestly, though, I am thankful for the beauty that has risen out of these ashes. It has been a painful transformation to live out at times, and my mind, body, and soul have known a weariness that is hard to describe. My experience at Columbine cost me something, and it has been emotionally expensive for my entire family. But I wouldn't change a minute of my story. Not anymore.

The very sure Hand placed on my back in the library at Columbine is tangible evidence that I will never be asked to participate in a trial on my own. It is hard *not* to have faith after experiencing that very real presence under the computer table. In my weakest moments when my faith has wavered, I have drawn from the revelation of that moment. Now I know fear and anger are not from God. The freedom I have found from those two things has come from the sustained peace and strength He has graciously provided to me over the years. There is no doubt that good is coming from the painful experiences that have happened in my life.

Certainly, though, there are things that I wish I knew more about. I'm human.

Hundreds and perhaps thousands of people in the world have questions about Columbine; I have some of the same questions. "Are you angry? How on earth do you send your kids to school? Do you think staff members should carry guns on school campuses? Do you think the media plays a part in these atrocities? How do you talk to your children about what happened to you? Have you forgiven the shooters? Do you think the police acted appropriately at Columbine?" I'm not an expert on any of these issues just because I survived a school shooting. But I have my opinions, just like everyone else.

Although I am sometimes tempted to mire in a pool of anger, I don't choose it very often. For me, anger is simply a choice, and it is a choice that feels exhausting. If I had decided to spend the last twenty years swimming in anger and bitterness, I would have been too drenched in misery to fully enjoy all the gifts I have received as well as the triumphs I have experienced along the way. I'm thankful to God for helping me cut a new path through some pretty deep waters.

People notice that I rarely use the names of the Columbine shooters; I prefer not to. I'm not sure why it is customary for the media to give killers household names after committing such hateful acts of violence. It seems like all the attention these shooters receive through media outlets gives incentive for others flirting with the desire to commit similar acts of hate. The sick way they think makes them believe they will surely be famous, receiving the twisted attention they crave.

Following a local news interview I gave, my oldest daughter Mallory asked me:

"Mommy, are you famous?"

"Ha, no sweetie, why do you ask?"

"Well, my friend at school says you were on TV."

"Oh, well, Mommy is on TV sometimes, but I'm not famous. I'm not on TV for any reason that people *want* to be on TV."

I feel strongly that the stories the general media should be discussing are the lives that were taken too soon. Those are the precious faces that should be receiving attention on television. People left to sit in heavy grief over their losses deserve public gestures of love and compassion, not racy stories about killers' backgrounds and perceived motives. In home videos, the Columbine shooters made it clear that they knew their names would be household terms; they *wanted* this, and the media gave it to them.

To this day, the media continues to cover killers' life stories incessantly after every tragic event. I wish they understood how this type of coverage rubs coarse salt into the wounds of survivors.

When I visited the campus of Virginia Tech days after that incident and stood at the memorial for all the victims, I felt ashamed that I already knew the name of the shooter. As I looked at the names of each victim, they were all new to me. That should simply never be so.

It is for all these reasons that the Littleton, Colorado community built the Columbine Memorial. My family was sent an invitation to join the planning efforts, but I felt it was not our place to make any of the design decisions; too many people had been impacted more severely than we had, and I believed those families deserved most of the input. The Columbine Memorial is truly beautiful. The lovely stones engraved with the stories of each person who died are significant representations of the precious lives that were lost; they are unique to each person, just as they should be.

The Wall of Healing includes quotes from people within the greater community and messages directed toward the injured and their families. For example, one tribute reads, *We remember every parent who battled depression and grief, anger, and sorrow; who battled the relentless task of waking up knowing their child would not come home. We remember every parent, every friend who spent countless hours in dozens of hospital rooms and bedside vigils, in the slow and painful process of recovery. We remember our pain, we remember our sorrow, we remember our heroes. We remember those who in sacrificial dedication risked all in time of crisis and need.*

These are the stories and messages that should be the focus after such tragedies; messages that touch the hearts of all those whose lives have been changed forever. Recently, I received a letter inviting me to take part in the planning of the twentieth anniversary event set for 2019. I sincerely appreciated the invitation. I am thankful that the memory of those dear people who were killed as well as the stories of the wounded continue to be honored in the local community.

I have only been to the Columbine Memorial once. Patrick and I left Corban at home with my mom and took our three daughters for a visit with some other family members. We had been fielding questions from Mallory about what had happened to my arm. We have never lied to our kids when they ask about my injuries; we have only provided age-appropriate answers. These conversations feel completely impossible to me and my heart breaks each time they arise. I truly wish my kids would never have to know that their mom faced attempted murder. I never want knowledge of hate and evil to enter their tender hearts and innocent minds.

One of the answers I had given Mallory was in response to her question about how my arm got hurt. I told her,

"When I was in high school, two boys made some very mean choices. They hurt me and some other kids very badly." She seemed satisfied with my answer at the time. Patrick and I knew the girls were too young to understand the full scope of meaning at the memorial site and all that it represents, but we still felt compelled to visit. I will never forget watching Mallory's demeanor as we spent time walking on the grounds; she was only seven. My sweet and contemplative girl spent a long time reading each individual memorial stone and every single quote on the Wall of Healing. I was in awe of the situation unfolding before me; it felt completely surreal. She had no idea that I was part of the events she was reading about, but she instinctually reacted in such a somber way to all the things she was observing. We allowed her as much time as she wanted to spend at the site on that beautiful summer evening.

On the drive home, Mallory started asking questions I did not want to answer. Tears flowed down my cheeks as I responded to her, my heart wishing she never had to know that her mom was one of the victims she had read about. Mallory said, "Why did the boys decide to do that? What kinds of injuries do the people have who survived? That was really sad, Mommy." But, the most interesting question she posed was, "Mommy, what happened to the two boys who did that?" Deep breaths. I suppose I could write another book about my attempt to navigate these difficult details with our precious children. The process is still overwhelming to me emotionally. But I hope to be intentional, approaching hard subjects with grace and gentleness so as not to instill fear in my kids as they slowly grasp my past.

Not long ago, Ms. Klebold, the mother of one of the shooters, released a book. Many people wanted to know how I felt about that. Again, I had news stations around the country calling to get a reaction. I agreed to only one interview with Anne Trujillo, a local Denver news anchor whose dad was one of my oncology patients before he passed. Anne had covered a story about my nursing career six years after the shooting. I agreed to her interview because she did not want a "dramatic" news clip; she instead wanted to focus on something positive.

I watched Ms. Klebold's interview on *Dateline*, and I cried big, sloppy tears. It took me right back to that time as a teenager. I don't think I watched her interview or investigated her book hoping to hear a long-awaited, "I'm sorry." I still don't need to hear that from either family; they didn't shoot me. But I was genuinely curious about the content of her book. I remembered receiving notes from each of the shooters' parents about a month after the shooting. Ms. Klebold's letter was kind, gentle, and very genuine; the letter from the Harris family was brief. I know both letters were penned with words the parents never dreamed of writing.

To be honest, I cannot imagine the lives of the shooters' parents, and I have genuine compassion toward the difficult road they have walked since they lost their sons on that tragic day. I believe no loving parent sets out to bring their kids up to be killers. While I certainly think these two must have raised some red flags at home with their behavior, the choice to go on a shooting spree was the boys' choice, and their choice alone. The shooters even said as much in the videotapes they left behind. Children are not an exact extension of their parents. It is not my place to judge or tell the shooters' parents all they should have done to prevent the dark day at Columbine. All I can do in response is try to parent my four children the best way that I know how, teaching them to respect and value all human life, and to appreciate the authority of loving parents and teachers. I only get to choose what *my* parenting looks like. And, I hope it is intentional, thoughtful, structured, encouraging, and loving. I hope that it ultimately builds my little people up by enabling them to walk confidently as God's children, aware of the gifts they have been given to contribute to the world.

I shared these thoughts in my interview with Anne Trujillo on the local evening news. Surprisingly, I received quite a bit of backlash after that interview; a few in the audience questioned whether or not I blamed the shooters' parents for what they did to me. The response really hurt. I even reviewed the tape of the interview to see if I could understand the negative viewpoints. I'm a genuine person; there is not one answer I would go back and change. And yes, if I ever get to meet Ms. Klebold or Mrs. Harris, I would certainly have some private questions for them. Mostly, my questions stem from my role as a parent, on what they might do differently if they could go back. Their sons did attempt to murder me, so I think it is natural and logical that I have lingering questions. But there are those who think it is inappropriate for me to have any questions at all, that I'm not moving forward somehow; they think it indicates a lack of forgiveness. I don't think that is fair.

In my heart of hearts, I've never really struggled to forgive the shooters. I'm very clear that we are all in need of forgiveness. The bigger struggle for me has always been more about how I am going to let their actions impact my life. Perhaps more important than forgiveness was learning to make the choice to overcome the tragedy and not allow myself to live as a victim. There are times I do feel angry when there is something that affects my life or my family in a direct way because of their cowardly choices, but I am now able to allow the flashes of anger to go through me quickly. Then, I can purposefully choose how I want to use the redirected anger for good instead. We do not get to choose how people treat us, only how we choose to respond to their actions. How can I change directions? How can I reframe this? How can I learn from this? Those are the decisions I get to make that seem productive and help to move my life forward, not backward.

I believe most of my family members have come to similar conclusions. I have learned that watching the suffering of someone you love, though, can lead to emotions that do more harm than good if left unchecked. I can only imagine that if anyone ever harms one of my children intentionally, forgiveness will be much more difficult to extend. I like to imagine that if the shooters had survived, after getting over the fear that they might be able to "finish me off," I would be willing to sit in a room with them and attempt a conversation. I think more often than not, I'm thankful that it has never been an option. But I've imagined that scenario more than once because finding the goodness in all people feels important to me.

I am surprised how many people have opinions on how quickly I should have healed, or how I should have healed, or even what appropriate questions I should have in the aftermath of Columbine. The feisty part of me thinks, *When you come face to face with a mass murderer and survive, then you are allowed to have an opinion on my response.* There is no script that expressly states how each victim should handle the hard parts of their story, no matter how many years have elapsed. We are all entitled to ask the questions we want to ask, and all our journeys through the refining fire of life will look differently. I hope to extend grace to each survivor of a tragedy or hardship. As a lifetime people pleaser, I'm slowly learning to let go of contrived ideas of what others think of me, instead walking forward with confidence on the intentional path I believe God has laid out before me. I already have some thick skin as a result of multiple surgeries; I am growing it in newly exposed places now.

Gun control is not something I really want to talk about, yet it is perhaps the most common question directed at me. So many people think that because I was involved in a school shooting, I should automatically have deeply charged opinions about it. The truth is that I can see both sides. I sometimes wish I had some way of defend ing myself in the library. Something more than a chair would have been nice! I don't think anyone should be a helpless sitting duck just waiting for killers to have their way. But I am no expert; I don't want to be one. None of it feels fair or particularly right to me. The ways in which humans hurt other humans is appalling to me, as I have been a personal witness to it. Guns or not, why is every human life not cherished more in a country where we are taught to respect all forms of life?

I never initiated contact with the Jefferson County police. In the years immediately after the shooting, my questions about their actions that day rolled around in my head until I felt dizzy. My first thoughts and feelings were, *Protecting the people is your job. Why did none of you come in and help us? We were unarmed, innocent kids!* But my tune about all of that has changed pretty dramatically in recent years.

I think the reason most people enter into law enforcement is for the common good. I've met enough officers now to know that is true. The emergency plan in place at the time of the Columbine shooting did not support the officers entering the school immediately. Their command told them to wait; they followed their orders. I would bet every single one of them positioned outside the building that day in April *wanted* to run in and help us. In fact, I've heard stories from officers who speak of the battle they had in their own minds during those dark, slow-motion minutes. *Do I lose my job and just go inside the building?* At the same time, I think most of our parents would have run in without a gun or bulletproof vest to try to help us. Many have said as much.

I've been privileged to meet some first responders who were there that day. Almost always, when they find out I was injured, they are nearly in tears as they declare, "Please know we wanted to help you!" A few of them have even apologized. But there should be no shame. I have responded in various ways over the years:

"I wish you could have entered the building."

"We were told help was coming."

"I am thankful things are different now."

"It is okay; please know that. I know you wanted to help us."

I never want my response to cause more grief for these selfless people. They did what they were trained to do; it just took some healing and a more grown-up perspective for me to understand that. There are a number of people who left the field of law enforcement after that day; the scene they witnessed was just too much to overcome. That's true of some members of the Denver media, too. Of course, upon reflection, every one of the officers I've met said they would respond differently. Thankfully, policies have changed as a result of Columbine. No longer do officers have to wait outside for the okay to enter. They *go*. The bottom line for me is that we are all indebted to them for the sacrifices they make for our communities on a daily basis.

I cannot speak to how any other Columbine victim or family has chosen to live with the memory of what happened. I felt led to share my perspective, to finally give it to the world with the hope that someone else might be encouraged. If someone has experienced any of the things I have been through and finds courage and hope, this choice to be public with my story is worth it. I have never wanted fame or attention; those things actually frighten me. It is terrifying to share my most intimate details with the world. I feel completely vulnerable; my extended family feels the same way. But I've really learned through the process of writing my story that the fear of exposure is just another means of evil trying to keep the good from continuing to shine out of what happened at Columbine. I am no longer driven by fear, and that took years for me to be able to say. I hope I can approach each future struggle focused on growth and spreading goodness and light with my life. There's power in knowing that God won't leave me: He has never left me to navigate any of this on my own, even in my darkest moments.

AFTERWORD

I'm over my shoulder, in multiple ways. Some days, I'm leaning up against it. And on my weakest days, I'm still kind of crouching underneath its weight. But mostly, I'm thoughtfully gazing over it, looking toward the future. I'm thankful for this funny-looking shoulder of mine.

Hindsight really is 20/20. Steely resolve I gained from the year before Columbine made me who I needed to be to survive the massacre at the school. Steel is a funny thing. It's engineered by melting the pure element of iron with rusty scrap metal. In an extremely hot process that pulls out the impurities in the raw materials; it's an odd joining of junk and purity that leads to a much stronger product. It's just like my year before walking into the Columbine library, which got stirred up with my mostly perfect childhood. God knew what I needed to withstand the blast headed my way, and what started as a small fire in my life as a teenager led to a refining, altering blaze. I needed to be rebuilt before walking into that library; I just had no idea how much the transformation would hurt.

My parents often say that the year before the shooting was actually the worst year. When I spiraled out of control, my parents initially panicked. Should they have given me some space to figure out my problems since I obviously wanted nothing to do with them? Or, should they have given up everything to fight for me, knowing that as a teenager I was unable to do it for myself? The wisdom they demonstrated in deciding to obey a counselor's charge to "act like parents" no doubt saved my life. My parents made decisions to lay their own lives to the side to recapture my heart. I thought I deserved space to wallow in the dangerous pit of despair with my friends; I believed my parents were intruding and I hated them for it. I realize now that my parents were real heroes; they dug deeply and acted wisely even when those actions came at great personal cost. They went to battle for me when I was unable to battle for myself. By taking control, they helped rip the darkness from my life and slowly helped me to see the light again. I want to be a hero in the life stories of my children, especially when the going gets rough. Like me in my difficult teen years, many teenagers think they deserve freedom from their parents, but they are still kids who desperately need age-appropriate guidance. They do not always need the freedom they crave and demand; I believe they require protection and genuine tough love from their parents. I continue to draw heavily from my parents' selfless example in this regard in my own parenting journey.

And what a parenting journey it has been so far. I have been reminded that the wounds adults experience in their early years often get passed on to their innocent children. I do not want this to be the case in our family; unhealthy fear is going to stop with me. Of course, that all sounds rosy: it is much harder in practice than in theory. It would be quite easy for me, on my physically weary days, to place loads of blame: on the shooters, on the school, on the people who sold the guns, and on the police. And, I could certainly choose to live as a victim. But who wins in all of that? The shooters and their evil plan filled with hate. Not in my story, not anymore! Good will win in the end. Grace will win, too. That is the true beauty rising from the ashes that I have waited so many years to finally see. I may not have a perfectly working arm or hand, or even a pain-free life, but giving my children the perspective of what it is to truly stand victorious at the end of a long road of suffering—it matters. I plan to continue reminding myself of that message, speaking it boldly to others as long as I have breath in my lungs.

I have great hope for our smart and creative firstborn, Mallory. We are a lot alike. I used to be a little girl who really cared about what others thought of me: a people pleaser who never wanted to reach outside the boundary lines. I had a deep need to always look perfect, to be perfect. I have found freedom in realizing there is not one box that we all need to fit in: as people, as victims, as children, as adults. I've realized I want my kids to know that freedom. I want Mallory to know it is okay to be imperfect; having it together all the time is impossible. So much growth can come from being vulnerable and open to new ideas and experiences: I hope it does not take our oldest daughter the thirty years it took me to figure that out. True to form, Mallory has bravely entered the competitive world of swimming, showing real promise in the freestyle and butterfly strokes, as well as in the beautiful diving entry she executes almost effortlessly. I celebrate that she accepts hard coaching in her life to improve her skills. A bookworm by nature, she has also learned that hard work in school and sports opens doors of discovery that keep her happily engaged in the world around her.

For Logan Jo, I hope as a person living with a disability that I am able to demonstrate true courage. I pray that I can be an example to her of how to struggle gracefully, without allowing my limitations to completely control my life. I hope I can show her that I am not stuck in a box as a person who "just can't" because of my arm. I *can.* And she can. I hope she knows it is okay and even exciting to be different.

Of course, it was never our desire that Logan would have low vision, glaucoma, light sensitivity, cataracts, headaches, clumsiness due to poor vision, glasses, limitless eye appointments, daily medications, or any genetic condition that would affect her whole life and likely be passed on to her children. But we have slowly shaped new versions of hope for her as we are in the habit of doing these days.

The most recent version comes in little white packets of powdered medicine that she takes three times a day. Not long ago, we were made aware of a clinical drug trial at the University of Virginia (UVA) in Charlottesville. The medication is supposedly capable of lifting the "stop sign" present in the DNA of aniridia patients like Logan; it will potentially allow a reversal of the defect. I have always been hesitant about trial medications, but I did my research and felt more confident about it with each new finding. Logan was eventually accepted into the trial. God has graciously reminded me that the treatment for my hand and shoulder was cutting-edge, and now it is standard practice. How can Logan or her future children benefit from any new advances if patients are not willing to sacrifice time and money to blaze new trails with pioneering doctors? Our family counts this opportunity as a grand privilege.

The greatest hope of all is that this medication can help to stall or even prevent several complications that are expected to manifest as her disease progresses. Perhaps it will save her vision, or some of it, anyway. Logan has traveled to Virginia several times; these cross-country excursions are long, exhausting trips consisting of eight-to nine-hour days at the hospital for testing: staff poking her eyes, shining lights in her eyes, scraping cells off her eyes, asking her to answer hundreds of questions. Like the champion she is, Logan survives the uncomfortable testing and takes her medicine three times a day, never once complaining. The doctors and technicians comment during every visit that Logan handles the testing better than most of the adults in their care. An answer to our prayers, she is starting to own this experience like she is proud of it; she should be proud!

I hope as a family with two people living with disabilities, we can all continue to learn to have empathy and compassion for those who have not been blessed with great health. That is just a part of the human experience for so many people I have met over the years; I never want to gloss over good health like it is some kind of innate human right. I hope Patrick and I remember to care for other parents who work incredibly hard to keep on top of the myriad of "extras" for their kids living with disabilities. I often recall days when I have seen mothers of children with disabilities at a store, and I think to myself, *I know how hard some of your life is. I know the extra time and energy it takes to care for that precious child.* I love taking a moment to tell those moms, "Your child is adorable. He/she is precious. Trust me, you are doing such a great job!"

I hope our Bentley Mae continues on her path with the same confidence and freedom of spirit she has presently. I envy her, really. She doesn't fit in a box and probably never will. She is who she is and has no fear or hesitation about flying her unique flag. Many days, Bentley believes she really is an "Alicorn Cheetah": a cheetah with a horn and wings. She runs around the house using her cheetah speed! I would love to spend a single day inside the mind of our third daughter. She is wildly carefree, genuinely kind, and loads of fun; she also cares deeply for people and animals. She is desperate for her own horse, a desire I recognize. I've offered a Great Dane as a compromise, but Patrick flat out says "NO!" Bentley is magnetic; she is able to make everyone feel welcome and comfortable. I hope we can learn from her zeal and continue to enjoy each day to the fullest the way she does. I can hardly even imagine the stage of life Patrick and I are quickly approaching: three teenage girls living in the same house. Pray for Patrick; may he remain sane and calm as the estrogen levels increase in our home. Better yet, send him a beer!

I hope to raise our little boy, Corban, to be a godly man who really knows how to love people. May all his strengths be used to encourage others, and may he know what it is to build up the people around him. And may we survive the flying pucks that sail through our house as he practices for the real ice hockey he hopes to play, following in the footsteps of his dearly loved Grandpa Greg and Uncle Brett. Whatever he chooses to do in life—sports, music, art, business—I pray he doesn't let his career define him. May my boy be defined by who God says he is and how He directs his path. I have no doubt the three sisters that spoil him rotten right now will help shape him into an amazing husband who can genuinely understand his wife. Corban will be doing well to turn out like his daddy when he grows up: respectful, patient, gentle, funny, and fiercely dedicated to his family. He is sure to bring Patrick a lot of joy over the years as they play ball together; the same thing Patrick did with his dad as a child.

We are finally enjoying warmer weather full-time. Patrick and I had lived our entire lives in Colorado until the spring of 2017. While he enjoys snowboarding (well, he *did* enjoy it before we had so many kids), neither one of us is really a snow person. We are beach people! We crave the sunshine, the crashing waves; that is where we feel most peaceful and most alive. Colorado is an amazing place to live, and nothing beats a Colorado summer. But winters there seem to last forever; I can only handle snow for about a month. Thanksgiving to Christmas. But once Christmas Day has passed, the snow needs to go with it!

For years, especially on cold days, I whined, "I want to live in the Carolinas." And shockingly, now we do! The same week we learned about the clinical drug trial for Logan, Patrick accepted a new job. We had been keeping our eyes peeled for a new opportunity for a couple of years. We were not desperate for something new but just open to experiencing a big change. The traveling demands from Colorado to Virginia for Logan's participation in the clinical trial were going to be heavy on our family. It quickly became clear that God had plans to move us across the country. To our surprise, everything came together quickly and seamlessly. And did we ever appreciate it; moving four kids 1,600 miles away from the only home any of us had ever known was no small task!

Patrick was offered the new position of Executive Director of Tissue Services at Carolina Donor Services in Durham, a job that is close to both of our hearts. We are now an easy four-hour drive to UVA for each of Logan's appointments at the eye center and a two-hour drive from the beach, our family's happy place. Our children attend a small private school that provides us with great peace and belonging. And it is just the six of us for the first time in our lives. The solidarity has been a wonderful opportunity for Patrick and me to focus on the culture we want to establish in our family: a culture of intentionality, togetherness, and unity. Certainly, living far away from all our family in Colorado is painful and sad at times; we miss our childrens' grandparents' attendance at their school and sporting events as well as Sunday family barbecues. But we are hoping maybe one day soon they will join us in North Carolina! Nevertheless, it has been abundantly clear that this charming southern state is where God needs our family to be for this season in our lives.

Our Colorado families, on the other hand, are still mending their broken hearts; we relocated the only grandkids on my side of the family. Before we moved, my mom and dad told us repeatedly, "You and Patrick can go wherever you want to go, but the grandkids STAY!" Patrick's parents felt the same way. We know we are incredibly blessed to be loved by such supportive family members.

When we moved across the country, I secretly hoped that the "Columbine girl" identity I had long held in Colorado would get left behind in the relocation process. A new journey awaited, and looking back over my shoulder, I see God's handprints on all the preparation I needed to get to this new milestone in my life. At first, I very much enjoyed being unknown in the communities surrounding us in North Carolina. For many months, nobody knew anything about me, our family, or Logan's story. The anonymity was refreshing. Our family was known only as the Johnson family, without all the baggage. Additionally, the culture in North Carolina is quite different than the way of life we knew in Colorado; we have enjoyed engaging in a new setting. Yes, ma'ams and no, sirs! Over time, however, I have started to crave being known in a tight community again. It takes a lot of time to build that in a new state, especially when the demands of raising four kids take most of our time. We are truly happy in North Carolina, though, and trust that deep relationships will blossom for all of us as we continue to invest in our new community.

I trust that when my kids learn the entirety of my story, they can see the clear hand of God on my journey. I hope they will ponder the power fueling that Hand on my back in the library; power that is available to them as well. I hope my faith through various trials can show them how to persevere through hard times, and that examining their circumstances with wide lenses rather than tunnel vision is important. May they know how to seize the good that is available from each moment in life that initially seems impossible to overcome.

And I hope, like the earth bursting with growth all around us right now, we will continue to watch unexpected blessings sprout up from the dark soil of April 20, 1999. God has ultimately transformed the shotgun slug that tore through me into seeds that have grown to produce very good fruit in my life. The fiery missile of hate that burned through my body has not had the pleasure of destroying me, and what was ultimately meant for evil will continue to be choked out by all the beautiful good that is still to come.

ABOUT ALLOSOURCE®

Allosource was founded in 1994, five years before I was shot at Columbine. Since then, the company has evolved from a local tissue bank into an international organization serving communities around the country and world.

In the years leading up to its inception, three Organ Procurement Organizations (OPOs) throughout the United States recognized an extraordinary need: to replace tissues in patients with critical or debilitating conditions, while simultaneously providing respectful comfort and solace to families dealing with the loss of a loved one. This blend of medical application and human compassion provided a powerful solution. The organizations came together to create the only nonprofit tissue bank with OPOs as corporate members. AlloSource's mission was born and developed into a culture of commitment. *Inspired by the gift of donation from our communities, AlloSource responsibly provides innovative cellular and tissue allografts to advance patient healing.*

Today, AlloSource is one of the largest, most respected nonprofit tissue banks in the United States, with nearly 500 employees and multishift, 365-day processing. Over its twenty-five years in operation, AlloSource has remained a mission-driven business, committed to the wishes of donor families, the needs of their surgeon customers like Dr. Wilkins, and the hopes of patient recipients like me. AlloSource continues to honor every gift of donation by maximizing its medical impact; the focus on bringing progressive, compelling solutions to market is guided first and foremost by their commitment to industry-leading quality standards that never jeopardize a donor's wish or a patient's safety.

The employees working toward AlloSource's mission have developed new and compelling solutions while rein-forcing the organization's leadership as the largest pro-cessor of cellular-based products, cartilage for transplant, and skin to help heal burns. In addition to its proprietary technology, AlloSource collaborates with many compa-nies and creates products for some of the largest medical device and regenerative medicine companies in the world.

Tissue organizations sometimes struggle to find tissue recipients who want to share their story. Organ donation, by contrast, is often depicted in the movies and spotlighted in the national news; it is so familiar to the general public. Yet tissue donation often provides life-enhancing healing through a knee replacement or spinal fusion. The world does not always know about the life-changing possibilities it can offer to patients like me who receive these tissues. For instance, skin donation literally saves the lives of severe burn victims. Numerous professional athletes have received donated cartilage that provides them with prolonged careers. Bone donation saves arms, legs, and hands like mine, giving patients a new and often unimagined lease on a greater quality of life. I believe tissue donation is as important as organ donation. I am so proud to share my story of survival with the donation community and beyond.

ACKNOWLEDGMENTS

Putting this story into book form would not have been possible without years of encouragement, contributions of time, and advice from several people, and one special organization. Writing a book has proven to be more difficult than I could have imagined; however, being surrounded and helped through this process by so many who love me and find purpose in my story has provided me with great joy and healing.

First, my family . . . Patrick, our three daughters, and son. You have been the inspiration behind my desire to share a message of hope to others. My time at home with you is when I truly appreciate the beautiful life I have been given. Patrick, you have stayed up late with me so often as I worked through emotions, thoughts, and struggles while writing, and you have taken on more than your fair share of responsibility with the kids to free up my time to work on this project. You have been my biggest cheerleader in my growth as a writer and speaker, and I deeply love and appreciate you. Kids, your joyful laughter, snuggles, and loving hearts have sustained me through these past years, and I hope that this book will encourage you in your upcoming years as teenagers and adults.

It would not have been possible to fully tell this story without the willingness of my parents and siblings to allow me to publicly share their intimate experiences. Brian, Britney, and Brett . . . I will always cherish the hours Karen and I spent listening to you reveal your deepest thoughts and raw emotions about what you saw and endured during the year before Columbine and the years after. I learned so much about each of you, your hearts, and your loyalties during those hours of remembering together.

Mom and Dad, you have been incredibly gracious to me over the past four years while I have been writing this book. I know I have stirred deep memories and emotions. You have opened your hearts and shared your experiences as parents who have endured well while faithfully raising the four of us. Thank you for your devotion as parents. I appreciate you letting me expose pieces of our family story in the hopes that it will encourage others. Mom, thank you for the time you have watched the kids so I could write or edit. Dad, thank you for the endless hours you spent editing, reflecting and representing our family in this book. Without the love you two have poured into me, this story would not even be possible.

I want to give a special thanks to my wonderful friends at AlloSource. Not only did AlloSource donate bones and tissue in 1999 that were used to save my arm and hand, but they have continued as part of our family's story ever since. AlloSource coordinated my very public engagement to Patrick in 2004, provided me with an opportunity at numerous events to share the importance of bone and tissue donation, and believed in the message of this story enough to support my efforts to write this book. AlloSource is celebrating their twenty-fifth anniversary this year, and I am incredibly honored, humbled, and thankful to be a part of their story—an organization that continues to develop new and inspiring ways to impact lives for the better.

Karen Booker Schelhaas, you deserve a great big hug and "thanks" of your own. As we have written this book together, our friendship has grown even deeper. We have learned from each other, and trusted each other with the most painful and joyful moments of our lives. Writing with you has given us a unique experience as friends; an experience I will continue to cherish. I cannot wait to read your story someday.

The Schelhaas Seven . . . as a family, the seven of you have inspired me to continue to find joy, even on the hard days. You have cheered on your wife/mom, Karen, as she gave her time and creative writing to this story. You have been flexible to adjust schedules and expectations when the demands of writing were many. The Schelhaas family certainly has a special story of their own to share one day, but for now, thank you for being a part of mine.

To our editor, Anita Mumm . . . thank you! I remember sitting across from you in a coffee shop in Colorado as my dad and I told you of the plans to write this book. We were naïve and young in our book-writing experience. You were passionate, helpful, and knowledgeable right from the start. You have walked the journey of writing this book step by step with all of us. Your wisdom, creativity, gentleness, guidance, patience, and hours of work have proven to be invaluable in completing *Over My Shoulder.*

Krista Rolfzen Soukup, as my publicist, your guidance, knowledge, scheduling, and design ideas have been helpful in the home stretch of finishing this book. You have been patient with my questions, given thorough and kind responses, and have provided words of encouragement as we finalized the cover and website. Your passion for representing authors has been evident to me in your work ethic and desire to understand my visions, intentions, and ideas.

I would like to thank the rest of the team members who contributed to this effort. Katelyn Solich Photography . . . no one can capture the ideas in my head as well as you. Even when I was horribly sick, you were able to work your photography magic! Brian Smith, my web designer . . . your work is amazing. I appreciate your patience and quick responses as I repeatedly changed color schemes, fonts and pictures. Grace Kastens . . . before receiving your edits on the manuscript, I was unaware of the importance of a copy edit. Your work provided the finishing touch. 1106 Design, LLC . . . your work on the design of the cover and interior pulled this project together in a way that celebrates all the hours spent writing *Over My Shoulder.*

I could easily write a few more pages about the many others who poured their lives into my life as a teenager, survivor, mom, wife, daughter, sister, and friend. Thank you to all who have lent a listening ear or calming word as I have navigated how to best share my life experiences.

Love to all.
KACEY

ABOUT THE AUTHORS

KACEY RUEGSEGGER JOHNSON

A survivor of the 1999 Columbine High School shooting, Kacey Ruegsegger Johnson is a wife and mother of four, a national spokesperson for bone and tissue donation, and an inspirational speaker. Her story includes turbulent teenage years marred by the sudden deaths of several friends, a quick slide  into a deep depression, her own suicidal ideation, and the life-altering experience of sustaining serious injuries during the Columbine shooting.

Kacey shares details and insight into the devastating effects of depression, physical trauma, PTSD, and fear. Her ultimate choice to "survive to thrive" has led to important healing. Her recovery culminates in a newfound purpose and passion to share her story to provide hope and encouragement for others. Kacey's greatest joys are found at home with her husband Patrick, parenting their three young daughters and son, chauffeuring them to swim meets and hockey practices, and enjoying Friday movie nights at home in their beautiful state of North Carolina.

www.kaceyruegseggerjohnson.com

KAREN BOOKER SCHELHAAS

Educated in communications and devoted to freelance writing, Karen lives in Colorado with her husband Brant and their five teenage and young adult children, better known as The Schelhaas Seven. Hiking trails near their homes since 2006, Kacey and Karen first bonded as mothers nurturing their large families. Many years later they set out as book collaborators, combining Kacey's riveting life story with Karen's skill for creative storytelling.

Between jogging, cooking for a crowd, volunteering at schools, driving countless hours, cheering for her kids, caretaking, and traveling as much as possible, she can be found at her kitchen table in a cozy robe and fuzzy slippers with espresso running through her veins, thoughtfully drawing people into the front row of her experiences through the power of the written word.

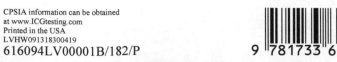